HALLELUJAH
DAVE

A STORY OF MISCHIEF, PASSION, AND HOPE

DAVID VALDEZ

WESTBOW
PRESS®
A DIVISION OF THOMAS NELSON
& ZONDERVAN

WestBow Press books may be ordered through booksellers or by contacting:

WestBow Press
A Division of Thomas Nelson & Zondervan
1663 Liberty Drive
Bloomington, IN 47403
www.westbowpress.com
1 (866) 928-1240

ISBN: 978-1-5127-6588-5 (sc)
ISBN: 978-1-5127-6590-8 (hc)
ISBN: 978-1-5127-6589-2 (e)

Library of Congress Control Number: 2016919424

Print information available on the last page.

WestBow Press rev. date: 12/1/2016

ACKNOWLEDGEMENTS

Although I have written journal articles and part of a chemistry book, this has been a very different endeavor. The emotional journey was an aspect never encountered with atoms, molecules, and reactions. I would like to thank the many members of my family who helped me;

My wife who encouraged me to write the story and proofread the manuscript multiple times.

My daughter Kristin who drew the cover of the book.

My cousin Rose, Otilia's daughter, who helped with the Prologue.

My sisters Lucy and Lonnie who helped me bring some of the stories alive.

My brother Phil who reminded me of some details that I had forgotten.

I wanted to also thank Mrs. Holly Viccaro of the Fannin County High School Art Department who introduced me to Lily Davenport. Lily was the artist for the illustrations found in the text. I would tell her the stories and her talented artistry would visualize with craft and humor the emotions that ran through me.

PROLOGUE

"I am going to America. No one is going to stop me."

By the time Licha was 7 years old, both of her parents had died. She had one younger sister, Mary. She promised her mom and dad before they died that she would take care of her little sister. Licha knew there was no future for her in Mexico. She washed floors, cleaned houses, and did any menial job to survive. Desperately, she would struggle at such a tender age. Fault this young girl for her brash insistence, she was coming to the United States. Nothing could stop that dream in her mind.

Licha and Mary were living in abject poverty as her relatives had little money to spend on these two orphans. Licha had a boyfriend, Felipe, whom she loved dearly but he didn't recognize her vision, her hope of a better life. At 15 years old she had decided to come to America. It was 1944, the War was raging across the world, but all that mattered to this little girl was survival and paradise to the north.

"I am leaving on the train tomorrow for the border and then I am going to the United States," Licha said.

"What are you going to do with your sister? I know you won't leave her," Felipe said.

"I talked with my cousin, Otilia. She will stay with her until I come back for her."

"You're not leaving, I don't believe you. We'll get married here," he pleaded disbelieving her daring plan.

"Just wait, tomorrow I will be gone. If you want to be with me, meet me at the train station." The next day Otilia walked with Licha to the train station at her insistence.

Felipe came looking for Licha. She was gone. She was not at her home. He scoured the small town to no avail. Had she really left? He raced over to Otilia's house in hope of finding her there. Mary was there with Otilia. Maybe she hadn't left after all.

"Otilia, where is Licha? What do you mean she is gone?"

Felipe raced to the train station. It hadn't left. He stormed through the passenger cars and saw her alone in a seat on the last car.

"Licha, get off the train!" Felipe ordered in a deep voice. She wasn't going to make a scene. She got off, for now. Licha knew what she was going to do. No one was going to stop this 15 year old, not Felipe, not relatives, not a silly river.

"Felipe, either you go with me or I go alone." He knew she was serious. So with little money and few clothes, they started their journey on that train to the United States. When they got to the Rio Grande near Laredo they tied a rope to each other's waist.

"If one of us drowns, we both drown. If one lives, we both live."

They managed to get all the way to Michigan. There in the fields they picked strawberries, blueberries, apples, and peaches. Soon they married. Licha was pregnant and Lucy was born in 1945 in the fields of Caro, Michigan. Seven months later, pregnant with her second child, she told Felipe,

"I am going back to get Mary! I have to. My heart is dying without my sister."

Licha would make good on her promise to always care for her sister. Felipe had a job, so Licha began her journey to Mexico with her baby in her arms, and some friends she had made. When Licha's attempts to reenter America with her sister were thwarted, she sent word to Felipe and he began his long trek to bring her back to the United States. A total of three times they had crossed the river. No longer would they go back. It was 1946 and Licha was now 17 years old. Mary was 14. They moved to St. Charles, Illinois. She had her second daughter, Lonnie, in 1946 and a son, Philip in 1948. So, begins my story.

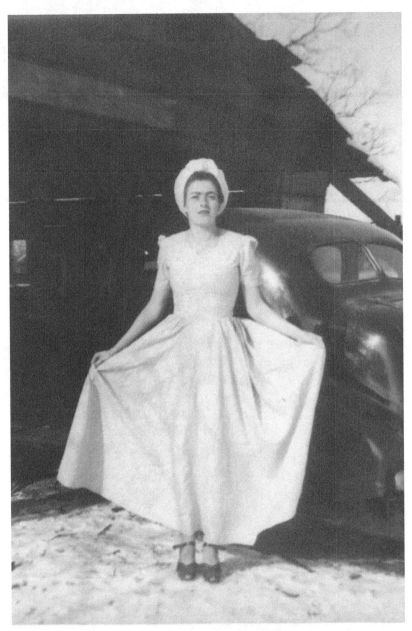

My Mother - 19 Years Old

CHAPTER 1

The Beginning

I recall somewhat vividly the day I was born. It may seem astonishing that the first major event of my life could be part of my memory. But it is, just as I am writing today. I was born at home December 1, 1949 in St. Charles, Illinois on the kitchen floor with my mother being the giver of this life. I am not sure if my mom picked the kitchen because of access to boiling water or maybe when the contractions came she just fell to the floor. How could I know that? Being born, being pushed and pulled is no easy task. Reaching for new life when Dad was about useless can be unnerving. You would have thought by the time he had multiple children that he would have known the routine. But no, there was my dad like most men, clucking like a chicken thinking he was a rooster.

I had two older sisters, Lucy and Lonnie, and one older brother, Phil. Lucy, the oldest, was upstairs in our two bedroom home. Our home was old and in disrepair. I don't know if you could call it a shanty. I didn't have much to compare it to but I knew we didn't have money to repair it. I suppose not many people did. A little past the top of the stairs was an air vent with a black grate. Back then they didn't have all that fancy duct work in the walls you see in homes today, just a large see through air vent from the first floor to the second floor. That two-foot by three-foot vent kept the warm air coming up to the second floor in the winter time as the old coal furnace heated only the first floor. Now my oldest sister Lucy at 4 years old was the most savvy of the bunch. She knew about everything well before any of us did. It's probably why she got pregnant at 16 years old.

Now my mom was going into labor and Dad knew we couldn't make it to the hospital. He got the neighbor to call the doctor and dispatched all the kids upstairs. And so therein begins my story with my sister Lucy stationed at the air vent getting the education of her life. Her baby brother was being thrust from the loins of our mom. And there I was scrapping away at new life; head, hands, and feet. Mom yelled and screamed like most women do and cursed the day my dad would touch her again. But once I was born, my mom cuddled me in her breasts and I fed for the first time. The doctor finally arrived and cut the cord. And there I was ready to explore a whole new world.

This was really Lucy's story, but she told it to me so many times that it became mine. I was there with Lucy, her arm around me, looking down at me being born, seeing with trepidation the most wondrous of all human events. Though Lucy tried to cover my eyes to protect me from seeing the unthinkable, I was there peering down through that grate next to Lucy, clutched to her clothing, seeing my birth. I don't know if this is rational thinking. But often I would go to bed and revisit this wondrous event that Lucy told me and I believed it to be real. I wanted it to be real. I wanted to know and embrace this event that others could never feel or touch. And here I am attesting to you that I was there upstairs looking down at my birth. I was there.

CHAPTER 2

St. Charles, Illinois

Now Dean Street in St. Charles Illinois is where I was born. It could have been the Sahara Desert or the Frozen Tundra for all I knew. But there it was, a dusty old dirt street on the outskirts of town. My whole recollection of the small house was two bedrooms upstairs and a kitchen and living room downstairs and a pot belly stove. There were three steps and a landing to get in the front door. My Aunt Mary lived in the trailer out back and she took care of us when Mom worked. Once every week we would get a bath. Phil and I first, and before Lucy and Lonnie would use the bathwater, we would have to clean the hard water scum from the tub. It wasn't uncommon in those days to share the bathwater maybe to conserve, but certainly to keep the water bill down. Not to be outdone, our neighbor, Lucy May, would wash her clothes in her small washing machine and then put the water in her sink to wash the dishes. What a clever lady! Lucy May was ingenious on how she kept her floor clean, too. She would lay down a set of newspapers on the floor and whenever it got dirty, she put another layer down. The Sunday funny papers were a hoot.

The first Easter I remember, Dad got us all baby ducks. It was not something unusual because we had chickens, a billy goat and my dog, Lucky, a big brown and black Airedale. I used to get on Lucky's back and pretend he was my horse. I loved that dog!

"Necessitan cuidar de estos patos." my dad said. (You need to take care of those ducks.) Well anyways, when we got our ducks out of the truck they all scattered in different directions like a group of kids playing hide-n-seek on a Saturday night. And the chase was on.

We screamed and laughed as we tried to figure out how to grab the ducks. Being the youngest, I wanted to ride on Lucky's back with a lasso in my hand. My sister Lucy, being the fastest, caught up to hers first.

"Papa, Papa, Lucy stepped on her duck and killed it," Lonnie yelled. There sat Lucy in the dirt with tears rolling down her eyes realizing what she had done. It's amazing that you can have something for only a moment and you can somehow become inextricably attached to it, remembering it your whole life. We gathered our ducks and surrounded our sister.

"Here Lucy, Here Lucy," we pleaded as we presented our ducks to her to cuddle and share. I'm not sure if we consoled her or not but we were all very close when we were young. With not many friends around we played, ate, slept, and bonded just like those ducklings.

CHAPTER 3

Batavia, Illinois

At age 3 ½ we moved to 209 Elm Street in Batavia, Illinois. Batavia was a small town of about 6,600 people and about 5 miles south of St. Charles. We were one block from the Quarry Park. This old stone quarry had been converted many years earlier to a swimming park. We swam, picnicked, and climbed some of the old quarry walls on the northeast side. There was also the Fox River just east of the quarry. There was this old one-person walking bridge that crossed part of the river to a small island. Half the slats of the walking bridge were missing and I didn't like it. You had to hold the side rails and gently walk across the few boards that remained. But there I followed my brother Phil, as I often did, as he was much braver than me.

McWayne Elementary School
Early fall, 1954, I was getting ready to go to school for the first time, kindergarten at McWayne Elementary School on the corner of Wilson Street and Route 31. From our home on Elm Street you walked west one block then took a right on Route 31. Lucy took my hand as we passed the Lutheran Church and crossed Main Street. Across from the A&P was the soda fountain shop just like on Happy Days. My mom would take me there and I would sit up at the counter and always order a cherry cola. Back then you got a cola from the fountain and then the soda jerk would add a touch of cherry syrup. The owner called me the Cisco Kid every time I came in. He could have called me Marshall Dillon or the Lone Ranger, even Davy Crockett. I am not sure if that was when I began to realize

5

that I was different. I had seen Pancho and the Cisco Kid on TV and as likeable as the two were, I began to see that people viewed me differently.

We passed the High School on the right and crossed the street to McWayne Elementary. The grass was well manicured and the fall air was pleasant. The anticipation was immense. I sported my best shoes and clothes. Before I left, Mom did as she always does, put her finger on her tongue and washed any last bit of dirt off my face and then relentlessly tried to push that cowlick down. As we got closer, Lucy stopped before we got to the door. She noticed something. She pulled me towards a window by the side of the building. A teacher that Lucy recognized was waving. As we approached the building, Lucy's third grade teacher from the previous year cranked open the window.

"This is my baby brother. Can he come to school?" Lucy said. The teacher asked some questions, nodded, and gave Lucy some instructions. "OK," Lucy said. "I will bring him to the office."

I was quite unsure of the whole process, but felt quite secure with my older sister. Lucy at 9 years old registered me for school and there I was in kindergarten beginning my formal education. Years later Lucy told me why she brought me to school and my mom didn't. She said Mom didn't speak a lick of English and typically the oldest child usually took responsibility when dealing with the English speaking public. And Lucy was good at it. She was beautiful to look at too, and the boys surely did.

Kindergarten was magical, playing with little wooden trains that I could only imagine owning. We listened to records of which my favorite was *Peter and the Wolf.* I could have listened to that record everyday as we lay on our nap carpets. I was very comfortable going to school each day with Lucy and Lonnie and then with Mom coming to school to take me home. We often shopped at the A&P on the way home as I was in the half-day kindergarten. Mom always seemed to pick up a cherry pie, my favorite, and sometimes a cola from the big red machine. Five cents in and out came the bottle from the bottom.

We seemed to have a happy family that included my Aunt Mary. She was slender and her hair was a vivid shade of brown. My mom was slightly older and when their parents died when Mom was only 7 years old, she vowed she would always take care of her sister. She would have never stayed in the United States without her sister. That was unimaginable.

By the time I entered second grade a lot of things began to change. I was a good student. I enjoyed telling Mom all I did in school. But something dramatic happened in second grade that I simply could not forget my entire life. We were going to learn how the postman delivered letters to our homes. So our teacher was going to simulate the Postal System. Simple enough. Everyone was assigned a person to write a letter. I wrote my letter, put it in an envelope, addressed it, and dropped it in the little mailbox that our teacher had made. The mailbox had a small slot at the top and was colored blue and white just like we saw in town. She distributed all the letters to a large box that was segmented into smaller individualized boxes with our names on it in alphabetical order. So we began. There it was, the first letter in my life written to me by one of the girls in class.

Dear Dave,
You are my friend.
I like second grade. Do You?
Amy

In second grade the letters are usually a little scribbly but her writing was impeccable. I was at the "Wow" stage of this game and this classmate assured me that it was going to be a good year. I cherished that letter in my heart. I don't remember if I had a puppy crush, but I do remember the feeling of presence, the feeling of worth and inclusion.

"Now, everyone write letters every day to whomever you choose and drop them in the mailbox and the postman will deliver them to your inbox."

We knew our teacher was the postman but we never saw her deliver the mail to our box. I waited for that next letter to come as I wrote letters to my classmates. One day, two days, 5 days, 10 days, and no letters in my box. And as everyone received new letters each day, my heart sank deeper and deeper. The only thing I could do was reseal that one letter from Amy and place it in the mailbox again. Every day I would look in my mailbox and the only letter I got was the one I mailed to myself. I pretended that I was getting letters from other kids in the class. But, I wasn't and the rejection was suffocating. I never really thought it was because I was Mexican. But I was just "different" and I didn't know why.

At home I always felt loved especially by my mom. I would take naps with my mom and when I woke up I would smile at how beautiful she was. Christmas was always an adventure. One year my mom opened a present from my dad. There was a can opener. Not one of those new electric openers, just one of those cheap manual ones. It was all metal and I knew it didn't cost much. My mom was so mad I thought she was going to throw it at him.

One of the best Christmases of all was when I was six. I came into the living room Christmas morning and found a brand new Radio Flyer sled with a beautiful red ribbon. The bright wood slats on the red runners and red frame looked surreal to me. That sled was fire to me. It was like the Mona Lisa to the artist, Newton's laws of motion to the physicist. Yeah, that sled was fire to me. I never had anything like that. Everyone wanted to try it; Lucy, Lonnie, Phil and half the kids in the neighborhood. We had a great Christmas Day sledding outside until big Rosie Spradley got on my sled. She went down the hill and over a little ravine and, "Crack" went my sled. Rosie Spradley sheepishly brought it back to me and small tears began crawling down my face. The cross frame member which supported the three long slats of wood you sat on was broken and the metal runners bowed like a cowboy's legs after a 10 day ride. My

Radio Flyer sled was irreparably damaged, incontrovertibly broken. We tried to fix it but my sled was never the same and the name Rosie Spradley never escaped me each Christmas since. Sometimes I am sad but mostly I laugh.

The Spradley's lived across the street from us. Lorinda was Rosie's younger sister. She was actually about my age. She also had an Uncle Tyrone who loved to hunt and fish. He would bring home rabbits and squirrels and skin them in the basement. He would hang their pelts up to dry. It was an awful sight.

Tyrone said to us one day, "You kids want to watch me cut this squirrel from head to toe and nail it to the wall."

"No Sir!" We ran out of that basement white as the ghost of Christmas Past.

The Spradleys always seemed to have a lot of food on the stove; chicken, mashed potatoes, corn. Maybe that's why they were all so big. In stark contrast, my sister Lonnie and I were skinny as any skeleton on Halloween. People often teased us that if we turned sideways, no one would see us. I once saw Lonnie sneak a piece of chicken from that stove and she ran and ate it. I think that was only thing my sister Lonnie ever did wrong.

Our home in Batavia had an old coal furnace. Every day during the winter my dad had to shovel coal into that furnace to keep the house warm. Then about once a week he had to shovel cinders out of that monstrosity. The coolest thing was when that big old coal truck came down our driveway and backed up right to the basement window. The driver opened that window and put a coal slide down into our basement where those big lumps of coal would come crashing down. He would lift the back of that dump truck until every bit of that coal was in our basement. When the dust settled, my mom would go down and clean up the mess. She had to, that's where she ground the corn to make corn tortillas. It wasn't too long after that, Dad got a screw type auger that automatically fed the coal into the furnace. It worked off a thermostat whatever that was. Dad liked the new invention as it saved him some back breaking work. He just had to order a fine grade of coal.

I don't know why I never really learned to speak Spanish fluently. I don't know that I yet felt different from other people or was made to feel ashamed of my heritage by anyone. We were the only Mexican family in Batavia and I always remember speaking English. My brother and sisters always spoke English to me and my friends always spoke English. Why would I ever need Spanish? But, as a young boy my mom and dad always spoke to me in Spanish and I replied in English.

"¿Que paso' en la escuela hoy?" My mom would ask. (What happened in school today?)

"Nothing, we played outside," I would say in English

"¿Donde estan sus papeles?" (Where are your papers?)

"Here, Mom," and I would show her my writing and worksheets.

Each day upon returning from school Lucy and Lonnie would bring new English words to the dinner table and teach my mom and dad the meaning. So we all learned English and I didn't really care to learn Spanish. I didn't want to. I just wanted to be like everyone else. We had friends like the McAdoos who lived two doors down from us. They didn't know Spanish. Their two boys were about the same age as my brother and I. They helped me learn to ride a bicycle on their big balloon tire bike. I don't know why they wanted to sell it. I think they were so excited to see me ride a bike for the first time they decided I needed that bike. My dad bought that bike for me for 50 cents and I was happy to have a dad and have friends.

Blaine Street School

In third grade I was transferred to Blaine Street School. It was an older two story school with a basement and playground on two sides. As I walked to school, I passed by a big stone building. I learned that this was Bellevue Sanitarium where Mary Lincoln was institutionalized after President Lincoln was shot. I wasn't sure if people still lived there but I was sure she died a long time ago. I was always proud to be in the Land of Lincoln.

I liked Blaine Street School. The best part was always recess and the classes weren't that bad. I remember doing well in spelling bees and math quizzes. I think most of the teachers liked me. I mean I was the only one who stopped by the West Batavia cemetery, picked up freshly cut flowers from the graves and gave them to my teachers. They liked them and when I saw how their faces lit up, it just energized me all the more. I don't think they knew where I got them and what difference did it make? Nobody else was going to use them. All that changed as I came into school one day, a little muddy from the cemetery and running in the playground. One of the fourth grade teachers grabbed me and said in the most horrible voice,

"You dirty little monkey, go down to the custodian's room and wash yourself off in the laundry tub."

She didn't say, "You need to go into the boy's restroom and wash your hands." She didn't say, "You need to be careful not to get dirty on the way to class." What I heard her say in my heart was,

"YOU DIRTY LITTLE MONKEY, GO DOWN TO THE CUSTODIAN'S ROOM" (you are not worthy of the nice boys room) "AND WASH YOURSELF OFF IN THE LAUNDRY TUB." (where all the dirty mops are, you filthy Mexican kid.)

I cried as I went down to the basement of the school. I washed my hands and then wiped my tears before I went back to class pretending nothing had happened. I didn't tell my mom, not my brother, not my sisters. I was different and I didn't totally understand why but I was realizing I was "Mexican different." I never brought flowers again. Those carnations, tulips, and roses lost their meaning. Though I knew I shouldn't take them from the cemetery, I just liked the smile they put on my teacher's face. But, something bad happened to me that day. Not something accidental, something deliberate and cruel.

My Heroes

I still visited that cemetery on Route 31. We always passed it when we went to the Dairy Queen in Aurora on Sunday evenings. The long lines at the Dairy Queen didn't bother me; it just proved how good it was. Everyone would get an ice cream cone, pile back into the car and proceed back home. I gulped my ice cream cone like my dog Lucky devoured a steak. Not a bite just a big gulp. I never figured why I couldn't lick the top and the sides and slowly enjoy a cone. I just devoured it like a frog on a fly. Mom always ate hers slowly, then gave me the rest of her cone. No one seemed to object. Maybe they didn't want a cone that somebody already licked. My dog Lucky licked me all the time and I didn't care. I was content on this best day of the week.

Well, in that cemetery on Route 31 was a huge monument and in front was a statue of what I knew was Davy Crockett. He must have been buried right here in Batavia, Illinois. But I wasn't sure why he was dressed in what looked like a civil war uniform. Every week on TV, I saw Fess Parker, I mean Davy wearing a coonskin hat and deerskin shirt and pants. He was my hero. But why was he wearing that civil war stuff in my cemetery? That was somewhat confusing to me. I was certain that Davy Crockett was buried there, convinced that he lay under that statue on Route 31 in Batavia, Illinois. When I saw in the final episode on TV that he died at the Alamo, in San Antonio, Texas, two huge issues sprung up in my little mind. How did they get him from San Antonio to Batavia, Illinois? I could deal with that and figure it out. I knew Lincoln died in Washington DC but was buried in Springfield, Illinois. But the second was impossible to reconcile. My hero was fighting those Mexicans, those bad Mexicans who were trying to take the land from the Texans, "the rightful owners." I had to put that one on hold.

So who was my role model, the Cisco Kid and his buffoon friend Pancho? Or was it Davy Crockett who died by the hand of Mexicans. I really didn't have any heroes anymore except perhaps Superman.

I really didn't want to go back to Blaine Street School ever again and was half-way happy when my dad told me that we were moving to Aurora. When I was older my dad told me that a group of men wanted us out of their town. Batavia was white and we were Mexican. My dad had told them he owned our home on Elm Street and they would buy it from him on his terms. So my dad negotiated a price and we left Batavia. No, I really didn't have any heroes anymore.

CHAPTER 4

The Move to Trask Road, Aurora

Aurora was another 5 miles down the Fox River Valley. Aurora was probably 40-50,000 people in size. We moved to a small home on the east side of town. I didn't know much about Trask Road but it was off Sheffer Rd, about a mile from Garfield Park. We had a small home with a well. You could go out in the yard, crank that hand pump and get the coldest water from that well. Now that was awesome! We were fairly close to Hermes Elementary School and if my brother and I chose we could cut through the fields in our back yard and be there in 10 minutes. But usually we walked the roads around the homes in the area to get to school. Mr. Hinck ran intramurals after school and on Saturdays. I think that is where I learned to love basketball. He was a great teacher. The best I had ever known!

We owned a couple of acres of land and we grew corn, tomatoes, squash, cucumbers and whatever would grow. We had an old red tractor with a crank handle. Someone would have to get in front of that tractor, grab the handle and spin it with all their might to start the engine. And putt, putt, sss, sss, bang, whoosh and that tractor would finally start like a bronchitis cough in the middle of winter. We had a cultivator attachment and when my dad got on that tractor, we would chase behind him getting worms so we could go fishing in the little creek we had found.

I remember our dad putting us out to work planting corn. He made a spiked stick out of a piece of wood. We would stick the spike into the ground as far as we could, push it to the side to open up a little earth and drop a couple of corn seeds into the hole. For hours

14

we toiled doing that. At age 9, I was not totally impressed with farm life. We had three small barns on the property, in two of which we had over a hundred chickens. Every morning Phil and I would have to take buckets of water and food for the chickens.

My mom showed us the deft art of wringing a chicken's neck. She grabbed that chicken by the head and faster than you could spit on your shoe, she would twist that chicken over one time. Sometimes the chicken would jump like a frog in a frying pan not knowing what direction to take. Other times it would just start running and we would all go chasing after it. Eventually all the chickens would drop dead and then we would gather them and take them down to the basement. There we would drop them into scalding water and after a little while begin to pull all the feathers out. It's kind of funny what a naked chicken looks like. I think it could be best described as Barney Fife in a nudist camp.

Now, my sister Lucy was good at this kind of stuff. She wouldn't get all hysterical about cutting up a chicken like some girls would. She would cut off the feet of those chickens and show us how to play with the tendons to make the chicken's feet open and close. Then she would open up the chicken and begin to tell us the body parts as we cleaned them out. She was one smart girl. She showed us the forming eggs of different sizes in the chicken. But, she never told us how to tell a male chicken from a female chicken. I am sure she knew but she wasn't telling.

My Aunt Mary and my cousin Peggy were living with us at the time. Peggy was about 6 years younger than me, not much more than 3 years old. I always thought of her as my younger sister and I am sure if anyone asked she would tell them I was her older brother. One beautiful summer day my mom was wringing the necks of those chickens and all of us kids were out to watch. I am not sure what it was about my mom scurrying around trying to catch a chicken. Her skirt flowing in the wind and her scarf over her head was a spectacle to see. It was like in the rodeo where a cowboy frantically races on his horse to catch the calf, ties its legs, and raises his arms in exhilaration.

David Valdez

Well my mom caught that chicken under the weeping willow tree and wrung its neck like a tornado on a mobile home. Now Peggy, calm and as observant as she could be, was sitting in a laundry basket, not far from where my mom was twisting that chicken. And there it happened, three jumps like that Celebrated Jumping Frog from Calaveras County, and that chicken was in the basket with my cousin Peggy. That little girl jumped and ran like she just saw the Headless Horseman from Sleepy Hollow. I am not sure if she ever calmed down but it's safe to say she didn't eat chicken that night.

Twisting a Chicken on Trask Road

16

CHAPTER 5

Hermes Avenue

From Trask Street we moved to Hermes Avenue. We traded homes and now we lived in a home with a regular lot, no more farming for me. I wasn't sure why we moved. I thought it was because we could live a little closer to the bus stop. You see, for work my mom would get up every morning, walk about a mile, rain or shine, and wait at the bus stop to take the bus to downtown Aurora. Then she would transfer buses to go to St. Charles, about 12 miles. This had to take about 1 ½ hours and then she would reverse the process every day. Now we were only one block from the bus stop. Mom had to be happy about that.

I met Clarence, a Dennis the Menace character, who was truly attuned to mischief. Now Clarence lived on High Street about two blocks from me. We would play football, baseball, throw snowballs in the winter. One summer day, Clarence had this clever idea. I would stand at the bus stop and he would hide behind the bushes across the street with several water balloons. We had our exact positions and roles practiced in advance. Well, there I stood with my hands by my sides staring down at that city bus as it came around that corner. Clarence readied himself squatting behind the bushes. That bus came to a slow stop with its air brakes whooshing. The bus driver opened that door and looked straight at me right in the eyes. Before you could say, "Your mama wears combat boots," through the driver's side window came a water balloon hitting that unsuspecting bus driver squarely around the backside of his head. That water balloon exploded around his head and shirt and when that bus driver stood up he looked like he wet his pants. I am not sure this was what he was expecting when he fell out of bed this morning. He sure didn't look happy. I ran faster than a water bug skittering down a 100 foot waterfall, not sure if I should be laughing or worried that my dad would find out what I did. He worked for the City Bus Lines. I guess I hadn't thought through that one very carefully.

Bus Stop Surprise

CHAPTER 6

The Casa Blanca on Kane Street

By the time I entered 6th grade we moved to Kane Street as owners of The Casa Blanca food store. It was a small neighborhood store that catered mostly to minorities, mostly Hispanic and Black. I went to Brady Elementary School and had a real mixture of black and white friends. There were some girls there that were really interested in me but I didn't pay much attention. My mom had a little sitting area where she could make food for the men of Mexican descent who came in. My mom made the best frijoles, rice, and tamales. My Aunt Mary made the best tortillas, bar none. They were awesome. Now tamales were a little bigger operation than the typical Mexican fare. One year, my dad brought home the head of a cow, eyes and all. I am pretty sure that they took the brains out but I didn't look. They put that head in a huge "olla," or pot in English, and cooked it for hours. Mom put the "masa" they made in the corn husks, filled it with meat, and rolled it up. She then steam cooked these tamales and my goodness, they were incredible.

We lived upstairs of the Casa Blanca Store. One of the fun things you can do at a store is look at all the coins in the cash register and find the really old ones. That is where I started collecting coins. One of the boys in the neighborhood would come in and bring in old V nickels and Indian Head pennies to buy ice cream and candy. I didn't think much about where he got them.

"My name is Dave," I said. "What's yours?"

"Thomas, but everybody calls me Fatboy Thomas."

"Why do they call you that?" I said, not thinking too clearly.

19

"I don't know, they just do."

Well stupid me. Thomas was very overweight and wore farmer bib overhauls with no shirt and no shoes most of the time. He never objected to anyone calling him Fatboy Thomas. What was he going to do? Fight everyone? And so we became friends. We played monopoly and card games. We always ate a lot, too. He even showed me how to take the bus all the way across town to the YMCA. There we would swim, play bumper pool, and table tennis. He was always nice to me. We stayed at The Casa Blanca for about one year.

CHAPTER 7

414 North River Street

How many times does the average kid move in his young life? I could have Googled that but what difference would that make. I mean Google wasn't even around and it wouldn't have mattered because I had no say in it. Here I was 11 years old and we were now going to our sixth home.

"Why are we moving again?" I asked Mom.

"Because it is best for our family." That was all she said.

My mom was a nice looking mom with a good figure. Her hair was dark and flowed down to her shoulders. At 11 years old, I was still close to my mom and had so many fond memories. Somehow it darted through my mind how I tweaked her breasts when I was about 5 years old. There she was standing before me and I was a little lower than eye sight of what I imagined were two of the largest breasts on this earth. I put my two little hands up in the air and grabbed her breasts like an ancient explorer seizing upon the new world. Did I mention that didn't go over real well? But it was my memory and it was crazy thing to do.

"Don't ever do that again," Mom scolded.

I sheepishly acquiesced and said, "Sorry Mom."

But I am not sorry now. I am not sorry for every kiss I gave her, every nap I took with her, every time I hugged her. Nope, not sorry I tweaked those breasts. It is my life, my memory and my love to you Mom.

414 N. River St - The Worst Home in all of Aurora.

I was convinced that our home on River Street was the worst in all of Aurora. As you came in the front, the second floor had a separate walk-up stairs. There were four one-room apartments and one bathroom that was shared by those tenants. I mean Paco lived up there. He had the biggest cowboy hat ever. He was that short overweight Mexican cowboy with the embroidered cowboy boots and a huge belt buckle. His hair flowed back over his ears like the mane of a horse and his moustache was cleanly cut like a Manhattan manicure. He had this awesome 1955 Chevrolet Bel Air with baby moon hubcaps. Even though I didn't drive yet, I could imagine myself cruising down Lake Street or Downer Place with all the girls dying to take a ride with me, maybe snuggle with me a little.

Cars seemed to always get me in trouble. Several years later when I turned 16, Jim Lautwein, my new friend down the street said,

"Dave if you can get the car from your mom I got a blind date for you and we can double date."

My mom had never let me drive the car alone and she was hysterical when I drove. She clung to the door handle as though she were on the edge of a cliff. Perspiration cascaded in torrents down her face. I drove afraid to look at her wondering if she was going into cardiac arrest. Thank heavens we lived right in back of St. Joseph Hospital.

"Please Mom, let me use the car just one time. What could possibly go wrong?"

"No mijo, just no and don't ask again."

But I knew how to manipulate my mom,

"All the other kids get to drive. My life is a wreck. You don't trust me at all."

After nagging for what seemed like hours, Mom relented and I was on my first date ever.

"You be home by 11, not a minute later!" Mom said.

We picked up Julie and Mattee and much to my utter exhilaration, Mattee was kind of good looking. We went to the drive-in movie and I pulled out a blanket. Mattee and I walked to the front directly beneath the giant movie screen and laid the blanket right down there in the grass. I was oblivious to the whole world around me though I am sure we were spectacle to everyone else. We made-out for the whole length of the movie.

As we were about to go home, Mattee softly said in my ear,

"I told my mom that I am staying at Julie's house."

And Julie not having said much to me all night fully content to give Jim 100% of her attention, bellows out in my other ear,

"I told my mom I am staying at Mattee's house."

I mean I might have figured that out. Why does a girl bring a pillow and an overnight bag with her on a first blind date if there isn't some outlandish female scheme? And so the incredible dilemma of a 16 year old boy begins with ...

"I am so busted. I can't take them home and my mom expects me home at 11."

So with a lack of common sense and nary a stitch of intelligence typical of the male species, we went driving. We finally stopped on an old gravel country road and parked, with Mattee and I in the front seat, and Jim and Julie in the back. The minutes stretched to hours and by morning I knew that there was a high price to pay for my first use of the family car. About 8 in the morning I came rolling into the driveway. I parked the car and I quietly closed the door. I sneaked to the back and I peeked through the screen of the aluminum storm door. My mom was sitting on a chair with her torso rocking so slowly. She looked like she hadn't slept a wink. I got a glimpse of what the life of a futureless human being would soon be.

"Where have you been? The police are out looking for you. You better start talking right now!"

Before the crescendo of unanswerable questions could reach deafening proportions, I sheepishly shouted,

"Mom, I know you are mad and I am ok." I threw the keys inside the door and I ran and I ran, out through the back yard, into

---

the alley, past Jim Lautwein's house and into the park. I didn't come home for a couple hours so she could rest and cool down.

Carlos and Maria

Now the second floor of 414 N. River Street was also where Carlos and Maria Montes lived. They seemed like the most loving young couple I had ever met and were planning a great future. They were both short and thin and seemed so perfectly matched. I would go up to their apartment with my sisters and as they talked I watched how he caressed and brushed her deep black hair. Later, I would ask my sisters about them and they just nodded and said, "They are in love." It was as though I could hear Carlos singing the song, Maria, from West Side Story. I hadn't seen many musicals in my life. They didn't seem to be cool. But, this was different. In West Side Story two rival gangs, the Sharks and the Jets are in a turf war in the middle of Manhattan. Tony and Maria are from opposite sides of this epic battle and they fall in love. Their love is so deep and when Tony sings "Maria, say it loud and there's music playing, say it soft and it's almost like praying," it was heavenly. I loved it.

I never knew Carlos or Maria to say a harsh word to each other. When they gazed at each other, time stopped just for a moment. I could only wonder if there was someone out there for me like that.

"POP" ... "What was that?" I yelled to my brother Phil. We both raced upstairs as we heard screaming.

"I was cleaning the gun, I was cleaning the gun." The tears were flowing full force down the cheeks of Carlos Montes. There Maria lay with a gunshot wound to the head above her right ear. His bride, the love of his life, lay motionless on the floor with Carlos inconsolably sobbing. I wanted to touch Maria and tell her it was an accident, and to please get up. Cher once sang, "If I Could Turn Back Time." And if I could, this once I would do it for them.

I never saw death before. Oh yeah, I had been to a funeral home, but I never saw death like this. The grim reaper came and stole all that was good.

First Floor – River Street

On the first floor of River Street is where I lived with my two sisters, brother, my aunt and three cousins. And on the other side of the first floor was a one bedroom apartment with a living room kitchenette. When we first moved in everyone on the first floor shared a common bathroom. Now my Aunt Mary, cousins Peggy, Jim, and Art lived on the front porch. I am not sure how they survived the Northern Illinois winters out there as there was no insulation and the porch was surrounded on each side by windows. They didn't have much more than a space heater. My room was in the hallway between everyone and the bathroom. Two bunk beds made out of two by fours and plywood with room for a person to walk beside us is where my brother Phil and I made residence at night. Nothing spectacular, it's just what we knew.

In the apartment next to ours were José and Delores Coronado. José worked and went to Aurora College. I saw those hefty books he read and I could not help but think what a juggernaut of knowledge he must be. Delores, his blonde modestly plump wife, was nothing short of adorable. Every time she saw me she would gush over me embarrassing my youth. No one was sweeter, more affable than José and Delores. José would take me to play some tennis. I wasn't that good but I was fast and was kind of the opposite of José. Delores would make us lemonade when we came back.

Basement - River Street

The basement initially consisted of a washing machine with the old classic rollers on top to squeeze the water out of the clothes before hanging them up outside to dry on the clothesline. And next to the wringer washer was the old oil burning hot water steam furnace. The clanging that occurred as the water heated up and flowed to warm the hot water registers upstairs was annoying but blended into all of the noises occurring in the busy apartment house. Now my dad built five rooms in the basement using cinderblocks where single Mexican American men could sleep. Wielding a ten pound sledgehammer, he busted out a hole in the front, put a metal awning over it and put in a front basement door. As you walked in, there was a stove, a small refrigerator and a metal table. Towards the back was a communal bathroom with a little shower. Here I was in the America we all dreamed about, in a home with eleven apartments sharing three bathrooms. At age 11, I was so aware of who I was and where I lived.

CHAPTER 8

Our Neighbors on River Street

Two buildings were adjacent to my new home. The first was the power plant for old St. Joseph Hospital on Lake Street. The boilers were loud and the only activity there was the random custodian checking the furnace and water pressures. More importantly, on the north side of us was the mushroom factory. Now to grow mushrooms you need a dark environment and a boat load of manure. Maybe that would be a great way to attract girls. I could call them on the phone. I think the conversation would go like this,

Dave: "Hey Mindy, maybe you could come over and we could watch a manure truck pass by. What do you think?"

Mindy: "A manure truck? You are kiddin, right?"

Dave: 'No, I am not foolin with you. The manure truck comes by all the time."

Mindy: "Uh, not today."

Dave: "Ok, Mindy, maybe next time."

Mindy: "If that's the best you can do, there's not going to be a next time. What are you thinking? Not today, not ever, you loser."

Dave: "Ok, Ok, take it easy, baby. I am here for you."

The mushroom factory was about a half the size of a city block and was three stories tall. It was abandoned shortly after we moved in and the building became ours.

Directly east of us was the Fox River. The Fox River is about 202 miles long starting in Southeastern Wisconsin going through the Chain of Lakes to the Fox Valley cities ending in Ottawa, Illinois as it dumps into the Illinois River. The Fox River was severely polluted in the 1960s from the paper mills in the North and fat processing plants in the North Aurora area. The release of toxic chemicals such as PCBs and the high consumption of oxygen by pollutants left the Fox River barren of most fish other than carp and some catfish.

My life at River Street 1961 – I was 11 years old

I started hanging out with Bobby Domingo. In Spanish, Domingo is Sunday and Bobby was everything that could be good on a Sunday. Bobby was deep brown. I can't tell you why I liked his color, especially in an age where white was loftier than all other colors. But Bobby was rich, his color was deep. I just liked Bobby. It's partially because Bobby looked up to me. I was a little older, a little faster, could hit a ball a little farther and Bobby would do just about anything to hang together. We would play ball at a field at Marmion Military Academy on Lake Street. Sometimes we would go to Solfisburg Park just to play other kids. We only needed four people to have a game, two on a side. Each team had a pitcher and an outfielder. All balls to right are an automatic out. The pitcher also played shortstop and thus pitched from the right of the mound as you faced home plate. We played pitcher's mitt which meant you had to make it to first base before the pitcher got the ball or you were out.

Now I think that Bobby and I were related. In my world, we weren't supposed to know who your relatives were, you couldn't risk anyone knowing that someone in your family might be illegal. Anyways, Bobby was just a great kid. His parents would lovingly call him Betto. Go figure. I thought Bobby was good enough.

Some of my greatest memories surround Bobby. Our families were going on vacation together and I was riding with Bobby in the back of their old Ford wood-sided station wagon. Bobby's dad began to spit out huge hockers out the front window, and they would come flying into the back window. Bobby started laughing as we got plastered and we wrestled, forcing each other next to the window. Now you might say how is that a great memory? How could it not be? Laughing until your insides hurt with your best friend. Yes, Bobby was my friend, my best friend.

Now Bobby worked hard with his dad who did upholstery in a little room in his small rented house on North Broadway. It was just north of Illinois Avenue right before the road curves at the railroad tracks. That house was so close to the street, I thought I would get hit by a car if I went out the front door. Bobby couldn't play much. I called him every day. I never knew why at 9 years of age he had to work every day when all I wanted to do was play baseball. You see Bobby was my hero and I was his.

Hey Bobby, you still out there? I haven't seen you in over 55 years. How are your brothers doing? Are your mom and dad still around? I still kind of miss you. Call me if you can.

Mom and Dad Divorce

By the middle of summer, 1961, I was 11 years old and my life was about to crumble. We had barely moved into our new "glamorous" home on River Street. Mom just had a hysterectomy and Dad was regularly coming home late. I didn't know why.

One late night I peered through the crack in the door between my bedroom and the living room. There I saw my mom slapping my dad worse than anything I had ever seen. My dad didn't strike back. He simply tried to deflect the blows. All over my dad's face was lipstick. On his collar and shirt was the crimson color of the kisses of a lovers tryst.

"Get out, Get out. Don't ever come back. Leave me, leave me." A little later I went over to my mom and tried to console her. I was old enough to know what was going on. As the tears flowed down her face, I could feel the convulsive sobs within me begin as I knew I lost my dad and Mom lost her man.

My dad came home the next day. My mom hadn't slept a wink. I knew she played and replayed in her mind everything that had happened the night before. My mom began to cry,

"You can have that woman any time you want, just come home

to your family, your kids." Mom's eyes became a torrent of tears. Dad didn't say anything as my mom fell to her knees and then on her face. She clutched the ankles of my father so tightly that the muscles of her frail arms quivered like a fevered child. She never looked up as she wailed,

"No me dejas, no me dejas." (Don't leave me, don't leave me) One by one my father unwrapped each finger of her hand from his feet and each time my mom's cries became louder. I was collapsing on the inside never before feeling the total desperation of a shattered heart. My sister Lucy had tears in her eyes but there was anger exploding within her. She raced outside and got in the car. Lucy was going to run that man down when he came out. At 15 years old, she was going to make right what he had made wrong.

Dad left without being injured. Mom and Dad soon divorced. I never even saw him pack his suitcase. He never came over and said bye to us. I never knew there was a problem until that day. All I knew is he had a new wife and a new family. Mom got River Street and the car, and Dad didn't have to pay a cent of child support.

"It's Dad on the phone," Lonnie said.

"Ok," I responded. Dad wanted to see me. I wondered why he was so interested in seeing me now. He never took me to play catch. He never came to see me at any school functions. He was never interested in my report card. He worked at the bus lines, and spent a lot of time at the downtown pool hall. That is what I remember.

"Mijo, you want to go bowling," Dad said.

"Ok, sure." Dad picked me up and to my surprise I had a great time and I was proud of the 60 and 80 score in my first two games. I was home in a couple of hours and my mom asked me,

"Did you like being with your dad?"

I said, "Yeah, I had fun, we bowled ..."

And then I could see the tears well up in my mother's eyes. It was those tears that I could read so clearly. *My husband left me for a younger woman and will he now take my baby?* I reached up and touched her, then kissed those salty drops as they channeled down

30

her face. And then I knew, yes, deep inside I knew that I would never go with my dad again.

Mom began working the second shift at Hawley's Products in St. Charles, Illinois. She had worked there since I was a little kid. She would leave about two in the afternoon and not get back till after midnight. Lonnie would try to take most of the responsibility for us. Phil wasn't listening to anyone by this time and I was beginning to make that same decision for myself.

CHAPTER 9

Junior High School 1961-1964

Summer was ending and I was getting ready for Junior High School. Freddie Barajas, who was the on-again off-again boyfriend of my sister Lonnie, was already going to Benjamin Franklin Jr. High School on New York and Blackhawk Street. Franklin was about 7 blocks from our house on River Street. He told me to come to school with him the first day and he would introduce me to his friends. He was going into 9th grade and I was going to be a 7th grader.

"The 9th graders pull down the pants of the 7th graders on the playground before school." Freddie said.

"No they don't." I said with a little boy scowl.

"Really it's a rough place. The older boys will pull down your pants and everyone will laugh at you!"

Now being a young 7th grader of 11 years, all I could hear was, "the girls will LOOK at you and LAUGH." Did I say I was a young 7th grader and could barely wait for my voice to drop an octave and join my fellow classmates?

"Freddie, you are one big liar," I yelled at him after school. He laughed and so began my school year.

I began to make some friends, Jim Truemper, Paul Hilliard, Lonny Hanna, mostly because we played sports together and shared some classes. Guy Tebbit and I were class clowns. They would invite me to their homes and we would mostly play sporting games. One early evening at Lonny Hanna's house, one of the guys had come upon some M-80s. We blew a couple off and that got boring. So we got a ½ quart mason jar. We lit the M-80, put the Mason jar over it and ran like a laser show, each one of us in a different direction. We all realized that there would be nothing but glass splinters and shards travelling in every direction. We all met in the back of Lonny's garage realizing that we could have been hurt. But, we weren't and it emboldened me for the future.

Next Door Neighbor – Mr. Schott

Our next door neighbor on River Street was Mr. Schott. There was a small picket fence wrapped with chicken wire that separated our two homes. We loved to play catch in our small back yard as I was learning to throw curve balls and knuckle balls. Sometimes the ball would get away from us and find its way into Mr. Schott's back yard.

"Get out of my yard. Don't come over here again," he would yell. So anytime the ball strayed into his yard we had to effectively calculate when to slither into his yard and recover our baseball. Nobody wanted to get the ball, so I was usually elected. Sometimes I would go directly over the fence while other times I would craftily make my way through the back of the lot.

"Get out of here. Stay out," Mr. Schott would drone unendingly. Nope, I can't say he was particularly friendly and I can't say I liked him much. So it wasn't long before we stopped calling him Mr. Schott, just Old Man Schott. He would get mad at my friends, yell at them, get mad at me, then yell at me.

At first I didn't care, but then this 12 year old just got tired of his grumpy nature. Something had to be done. We had this apple tree in our back yard and I surely thought that some good use could come of it. So I took some soft apples off the ground and I cored out the center with the pointy tip of a potato peeler. Down the center of those rotting apples I packed some blackjack firecrackers nice and tight. With a match I lit those fuses and lofted those homemade apple hand grenades into Mr. Schott's back yard.

"KaBoom, KaBang, KaBoom."

It was the 4th of July in the middle of August. I watched the apples explode into pieces onto Mr. Schott's porch, patio and backyard and I ran like a scared rabbit. One thing for sure, I was becoming a good runner.

I hid beside my home watching Old Man Schott look at that mess, raise his fist, and say the unrepeatable. I remember thinking, I won this time. I had beaten Old Man Schott, except for one major miscalculation. I didn't run far enough.

"Yes sir, Mr. Officer, is there a problem?" I said as I saw the tall policeman in his bright blue uniform approach me. His badge and gun didn't scare me but I was surely glad my mom wasn't home. That would have scared me!

"Your neighbor has reported that someone has thrown firecrackers at their house. Was that you?"

"No Sir, there must be some sort of mistake. Do you know what direction they came from?" I asked the officer.

He took off his hat and wiped his brow. He looked at Mr. Schott's back porch and then he looked at the apple tree. I think he saw my sheepish smile and had me figured out pretty well.

"Listen, Son, just give me the rest of your firecrackers."

"OK," I said. And I went in the house and grabbed about one fourth of my firecrackers. Surely, I couldn't give them all up. The officer left and I don't ever remember saying another word to Old Man Schott.

Mischief on River Street

A Pattern Emerges

As my 7th grade year at school progressed, Phil and I began skipping school. Phil didn't like school and I was just bored. We would mostly watch TV but at times we would go down to the river and just hang out skipping rocks or playing by the coal piles. One day, there was a knock at our door. It was Mr. Dorn, the principal of Benjamin Franklin Jr. High School making sweet inquiry of our situation.

"Yes Sir. Mr. Dorn we have all been very sick," my brother Phil whispered followed by a cough fabricated from the deepest recesses of his lungs. I popped my head by the door so Mr. Dorn could see me too.

"Is your mom or dad home," Mr. Dorn said.

"No Sir," we said. My mom really never knew we began skipping school as she was working.

"You are going to be at school tomorrow. Right boys?"

"Yes Sir, Mr. Dorn." I didn't miss a lot of days during Jr. High School after that.

The Mushroom Factory

The mushroom factory was almost a stone's throw from our house. No, it was exactly a stone's throw from our house. My brother and I knew that for certain. The mushroom factory was never well kept but after it was abandoned, it fell into major disrepair with many of its windows broken out by "unknown" vandals. The electricity had been turned off and anything of major consequence had been ripped out and taken. That is when I began to investigate the vestiges of that old building. At this time the mushroom factory was the last building on North River Street. It was several hundred feet long and three stories tall.

I would cut across the back of the lot behind St. Joseph Hospital to get to the back of the mushroom factory. I set up a plank and I got in through a second floor window as the building backed into a small hill. I spent a lot of time going through all the doors and floors of that building. The building was falling apart. The floor was pocked with man sized holes and the windows between the rooms were rotted through. Early on, the police caught wind that there were kids entering into mushroom factory. The first time they came I scrambled up to the roof and watched the squad car carefully. I didn't think they would get out and even if they did, they could never catch me in that dark drab building. I knew every turn and they would probably hurt themselves. In that building I began to feel invincible towards the police. I was much smarter than them.

I first began giving tours of the old building to Jim Lautwein, Rusty Ostreko, and Billy Garza. The tours began to expand and kids from school came by for guided tours. A dark environment was needed to grow mushrooms and there were places even in midday where it was hard to see even a few feet in front of you. On every tour I would warn each person to walk behind me single file.

One day after school, Billy and I were giving a tour, and two police squads came in front of the building. They circled a few times, stopped and got out of their cars. The two officers looked up and then walked around the front of the building. They were trying to figure out if we were inside. Some of the kids were getting scared and wanted to run. I said with a stern voice,

"Don't move and don't make a sound. They won't come in. They will leave as soon as they think there is no one here."

After about 10 minutes they got back in their cars and left. A few weeks later I found that kids were coming into the mushroom factory on their own and I knew that was trouble. I was the guide. I knew better than anyone else the daunting hallways and the darkened dingy passages. Not long after, one of the kids fell down through a floor and broke his arm. Another boy decided to climb the inside of the big smokestack. I heard the rung broke when he was about half way up and he fell to his death. The mushroom factory was demolished shortly after that.

Summer at the Pool

Trying to keep from being bored during the summers, I would often go to the West Side Swimming Pool. It was on Russell Street next to Holy Angels School. I didn't go swimming often. I just wanted to hang out, be a part of a group. Every day was a ritual. In preparation for the long walk, I would fold the cuffs of my jeans, one, two, three times over to show my white cotton socks. A cut-off blue jean jacket over a t-shirt completed a James Dean type look. He was the cultural icon of dissatisfaction and disillusionment, a rebel without a cause.

"I am going to the pool, wanna come?" I asked my brother. He never came with me. We had a completely different set of friends by this time. Phil was just more interested in going to Sterling where there were more Mexican girls. I was content to go to the pool on my own.

Every day it seems I would go. Sometimes I would be there alone, sit on a picnic table and stare almost as in a trance. I sat outside of the pool and would peer through the chain-link fence in a daydream lost in my deepest of thoughts.

Sitting on the red splintered picnic table, I let my fingers trace out the engraved messages of love, sex, and subliminal persuasions. And there of course was the universal message of all graffiti, "if you need sex, call this number." Who the is gonna answer that phone, I think.

"Karate kick, wanna karate kick. C'mon Dave," Tom yelled.

I didn't really want to kick somebody in the rear or worse yet in the groin. Think about it. These kids spend half their day trying to look buff and then the other half they want to go kick each other in the groin. What fun is that? But, I played anyway; slap, punch, and get kicked in the groin. Slap, punch, get kicked in the groin. The absolute idiocy was astounding, but there we stood in sheer stupidity. I waited for more kids to come and join my daily routine.

"Diane, Debbie, over here," I yelled. What a pair. They're like me I thought to myself, kindred spirits. Never off the edge, just close to it. Now Debbie was young but had all the attributes of a well-made woman. As she walked towards me I pretended not to notice the way she moved, each wiggle, each bounce of flesh. She put my pheromones on red alert.

"Hi, Dave," Debbie cooed and I began to slowly melt into my shoes. I looked down and hoped that I was not a pool of goo. I looked up slowly stopping to gaze a little longer where I shouldn't. I was a mess as her light brown hair was beautiful and her face radiated like the sun through forest greens.

"Been here long?" and I am captivated by the motion of her deep breath.

"Nah, just got here," I lied. And I tried to talk to her a little longer but the only thing I could think of was "amazing" as I stared.

Now Diane, not as stunning as Debbie, but her blond tresses parted in middle, curled at the shoulders, still teased me in the wind. Introspective, deep, lanky, just like me, I liked Diane. Maybe because Debbie I could only dream of but Diane could be mine.

"Diane, go for a walk?" Diane was taller than Debbie and she walked with her elbows and knees bouncing like a marionette at the hands of an expert puppeteer. By no means was this a criticism, I loved the way she walked.

We talked about simple things as her hair wisped in the wind, "My uncle is commissioner in town." I didn't tell her that my brother-in-law was in jail. Relentlessly, I gazed at her, counted every shining tooth, perfect. I felt the sun glitter off her hair and it warmed me gently beckoning me a little closer to her side. I glanced at her new shoes, loafers neatly polished, and for a moment I was ashamed of my own. On impulse, I wanted to hold her but I couldn't.

"Yeah, I live on Lancaster Boulevard," she said smiling my way. And though I longed to kiss her, I didn't. Why did we have to talk about where we lived? When Clare came over last week, behind her on the wall there was a cockroach. Not any cockroach, a HUMONGOUS cockroach of gargantuan proportions. I tried to distract her to the left and the cockroach moved left, to the right and the cockroach moved right. Am I a person so cursed that when Clare Petersohn, a beautiful Scandinavian girl who has somehow overlooked this house on River Street comes over that a cockroach has to insert itself into my conversation and my book? I felt my whole body slither onto the floor. God, take me now, I thought.

Maybe to get my attention, maybe not, Diane's hand softly

brushed across mine. I craved the energy that ran down my hand hoping it would never end. Clumsily, I stumbled over the buckled sidewalk, embarrassed by the awkward surge of my body, embarrassed that eons of silence had somehow drifted between us on our walk. I shrugged my shoulders as we crept back to the park in a slow deliberate stroll. I hoped to say something profound to Diane, something to make it right. As we reached the park I blurted out,

"Everybody's lookin for somethin." I walked away thinking about what I had said and if I should wash my jeans tomorrow.

CHAPTER 10

Fox River Adventures

The Fox River was always of special fascination to me. We would make rafts from log scraps we found along the river. We tied them together and then made outriggers to stabilize the raft. With a long pole we would venture up and down that river always remembering to stay away from the dams. In the winters when the river froze over, we would walk across the ice near the Illinois Avenue Bridge. It was about 200 feet across. It was unnerving at times to hear the ice crack and listen to the echo travel up and down the river.

One winter when I was in high school, we had this incredible idea. We were down by the North Avenue Bridge with the dam slightly upriver from us. The river divided at that point around Hurd Island. There, the current was a little faster so it took a little longer into the winter for the ice to form and it also caused the ice to thaw a little earlier in the spring. Rusty Ostreko and I had an idea. We told our plan to George and Neal and everyone was in! As there was a thaw going on, there were sheets of ice protruding out into the river right under the bridge. We went to my sister Lonnie's house on Broadway and grabbed a few bats and shovels. We came back and began to cut out a piece of ice. We were going to ride a sheet of ice down the river in the middle of winter. This was incredible.

"Its breakin free, It's breakin free." Neal, George, and Rusty were on the sheet of ice as it broke free. I jumped from the shore and grabbed the edge of the ice sheet with my feet dangling in the freezing water.

"Help me!" I yelled. They extended a shovel handle and I pulled myself aboard. Here we were, four guys floating down the river screaming in exhilaration. Suddenly, our weight began to cause the ice sheet to crack. Our float was going down and we were going with it.

"Jump, everybody Jump!" Rusty was screaming. The water was ice cold and we were in about chest high navigating ourselves back to shore.

"Hot Dog, what a rush!" Neal shouted. We headed back to my sister Lonnie's house not with the idea of simply drying off. We had to do it again. About an hour later, we were back down at the river. Sometimes you can't cure stupidity and today we were living proof.

"We have to carve this one out a little bigger," Rusty said. Rusty had found a long pole so that when we got out onto the river, he could direct the ice float. The first time our ice sheet was about 12 feet by 12 feet. We were convinced that we needed a 15 feet by 15 feet sheet to hold our weight. Rusty surveyed the potential areas where we would make the next incision. A little further upstream we drew the outline onto the ice. It took us about an hour to cut through and this time I was on board when we broke free. Down the river we went. As I looked back at the North Avenue Bridge, I wondered if people gazing out of their car windows were amazed at what we were doing. Or maybe they thought, we were just plain idiots. Undoubtedly the latter.

After a quarter of a mile down the river, the current picked up and ice was building up along the shore. It was going to be difficult to get back to shore. If we fell in, we would have to pull ourselves up over the ice that protruded from the shore to get back on land. I am sure the other guys were thinking the same thing. Another quarter of a mile and sheer panic was setting in. I am not sure if we were screaming or if there was complete silence. Either way there was something profound about this moment. Maybe the guys in a platoon or a fighter plane felt that same emotion that came from knowing that we would all experience the same fate. Maybe it was something that would bond us forever.

As we went further down the river, there was a railroad trestle over the river that was anchored by huge concrete pylons. Rusty was directing our journey with his pole. When he realized that we had to make a decision, he yelled,

"Everyone get in a line, we are going to crash into the pylon and one by one jump up on it." Single file we jumped onto this 12 foot pylon that projected into the current in the middle of the river. There we were, four guys on the pylon in the middle of nowhere. We looked up and had to devise a way to get to the top to the railroad tracks. We boosted each other up one by one from the concrete pylon to a cylindrical concrete base that stabilized the arches of the bridge. Our hands were frozen and our skin felt like it was cracking as we then climbed into the arches beneath the bridge.

Railroad Bridge on South Side of Hurd Island

"Hang on," I yelled, "Just do it or I am gonna whip you right after we get out of here." Now how does that make sense? If you fall off into the river and break an arm or worse yet drown, I am going to beat you to an ugly pulp. But to us, we knew the danger and urgency of our situation. Slowly, we found each foothold and pulled ourselves up through the arches and onto dry land.

It was many years later that I met Rusty Ostreko's son. I introduced myself to him and he squinted at me and began to ask,

"Did you and my dad ..."

I didn't let him finish. I said "go down the Fox River on an ice float. Yes we did and here is our story."

CHAPTER 11

Mom Remarries Twice

Somewhere intertwined with my growing up, my mom remarried twice, both for short periods of time. Mom first married Cliff, a towering Norwegian. Everyone in his family was tall. I liked Cliff and he liked me. He took a genuine interest in me, more than I remember my father doing. He would take me to Sears shopping for plumbing supplies, tools, just about anything. We would be a mess, dirty from working. He said,

"You never lose respect coming in dirty to a store if you have been working hard." I always remembered that.

He had a huge laugh and a Minnesota accent. I was crushed when Cliff left. Mom and I picked up the pieces. Then Mom began seeing Carl. I didn't like Carl but Mom married him anyways. She insisted that he would take care of us if anything happened to her. I deeply doubted that. Carl was different, the kind of difference that never let us develop any kind of relationship. Mom and Carl divorced. I didn't care.

Likewise my dad had remarried and divorced. Many years later when they were both single, they decided to get back together again. Dad forgot the 8 years he was gone and tried to tell me how to live my life as though he was there for me the whole time. One time I had returned from a major rock event, Goose Lake International Music Festival in Michigan, where over 200,000 kids had partied and camped in a field. The concert lasted for 3 days. Joe Cocker, Jethro Tull, Bob Seager, Alice Cooper, and The Flying Burrito Brothers were just some of the bands. My buddies and I had picked up cheap wine and had barely anything to eat for the entire weekend. The drugs for sale were plentiful. I got home Sunday evening and I sat with the family watching the news on TV. There was a story and a newscast from a helicopter fly over of the festival.

"That's where I was, that's where I was!" I yelled as I pointed out on the TV screen the exact location where we sat. My dad sat there so angered at me I thought he was going to explode. He began telling me things were going to change.

"You are going to go where I tell you to go, and do what I tell you to do and that's it!" commanded my dad. I sizzled inside.

"Too bad there wasn't someone telling you what to do cause if you would have listened, you would have never left my mom." Some very ugly words were exchanged that night and he came at me. I ran out the door with him chasing me. He wasn't going to catch me. As I said before I got good at running. After my mom died in 1985, I wrote this story-poem.

Mama Said Hush Child
There are colors in the web of light I do not yet understand ...

I barely remember waking up through the commotion and confusion. I peeked through the slit in the door that spilled light into my room. "Mama, No!" I said as she flailed on the soul and body of my father; arms flying, head jerking, voice cracking. Papa stood expressionless, motionless in a world I could not comprehend.

Lipstick on his face, lipstick on his collar, shirt, back everywhere. I don't know why Papa had to come home like that. Maybe he wanted to get caught. Maybe she wanted Mom to know. But I know now – there are steps that pass through every corridor and the doors that lead the way. And tonight the evening wind blew a squall of tears through the corridors of my life and the doors that haunt my mind.

"Hush Child," Mama said. "It will be OK."
"Hush Child," she said. "It will be alright."

Mama wailed and cried.
But to me she said,
"Hush Child, it will be OK."

Don't go see your father. Tell him NO! Mama's burning tears
were crystals of ice freezing me from a world I loved. I felt fragile
emotions tied to the heart of a child crash to the floor, like a web of
light through stained glass windows.

I cry the quiet tears
That never go away.
Afraid to tell you how I feel,
Afraid of what you'd say.

Now Mama married the greatest guy, a Norwegian named Cliff.
Tall as I could stretch my hands and add a whistle and a laugh. He
painted on me the smiles of a child, kaleidoscope eyes with colors
that prisms shear. He made me a go-kart that drove the tears away.
And Cliff left.

"Hush Child," Mama said. "It will be OK."
"Hush Child," she said. "It will be alright."
Mama wailed and cried.
But to me she said,
"Hush Child, it will be OK."

I'm marrying Carl. If anything happens to me, there is someone
to care for you. But why? I am old enough to take care of myself.
Why? To fetch him stuff when he yells my name. And Carl left.

There are no tears
In a well that's dry.
There is no home
When a soul can't cry.

You got back with Dad. How is it that the same spectrum of colors can shade two souls so differently? But you loved him and we knew that. But now Mama, Dad left again, and you are on the bed and the shadows come. Doctor said, "Pancreatic Cancer, Whipple Procedure, maybe save your life." We knew better. Now everyone's crying and you are asleep in my sister's room. The ambulance came to pronounce you dead. Mama, there are so many colors in the web of light. Some I have never known.

"Hush Child, It will be OK."
"Hush Child, It will be alright."
Everybody wailed and cried.
But I said to myself,
"Hush Child, it will be OK."

CHAPTER 12

High School Years 1964-1967

I began high school at West Aurora High School at the advanced age of 14 years old. I was a sophomore as the high schools in Aurora spanned only 3 years. I started skipping school again. I would be absent at least once each week and sometimes both on a Friday and a Monday. I could only think that I needed a day to prepare for the weekend and a day to recover from it. My Latin teacher, Mr. Evers, began to call me Sunflower because he said I only came to school when the sun was out. Somehow, I was able to keep up with my studies half-way respectably. I hated honors Geometry; I hated all the honors classes. The kids in there were not my close friends. They had friends of their own choosing. I used to write my own excuses for my absences and sign my mom's name. I was getting good at forging it. I even forged Jim Truemper's dad's name once and that was tough. It had so many swirls.

But, the gauntlet was finally thrown down. Late January, I got a note from the office that my counselor, Miss Tisher, wanted to see me.

"David, I have been meaning to talk to you about your attendance. Do you know how many days you have missed this year?" she asked.

"No Miss Tisher, not many I think," knowing full well that I had skipped days to go fishing, to go ice skating, and just watch daytime TV.

"You have missed 30 days."

"30 days?" I said incredulously. "But, my grades are still ok." I think to myself, that's only skipping about 1 to 1 ½ days per week. How can that possibly be a problem?

"Do you know what's going to happen if you miss any more?"

"No Ma'am," I said in my most respectful tone.

"We are going to flunk you for the whole year. And then you will be suspended for the rest of the year. Is that what you want?"

"No Miss Tisher," I said thinking she really means business. I had these great hopes about one day attending college like I saw José Coronado do.

"So will I have to see you in this office again," Miss Tisher said in a much softer tone.

"No Miss Tisher," I said. So I began to go to school. It is amazing that if you go to school every day and listen that you can actually improve your grades. It was about this time that I began to hear other students seriously talk about going to college and I was interested. I had no idea what the process was or who to ask.

Physics, taught by Mr. Pinnow, came along in my junior year and that just seemed easy. I never studied much but I began helping my friends. One time Brian Carson invited me over to his house after school. As we studied, his mom brought us over cookies and milk. I remember that she was very friendly but I couldn't get over that for no apparent reason she brought us this delicious snack. I couldn't figure if this was normal or not. Maybe if she yelled out from the kitchen,

"If you two bean poles want a snack, help yourselves in the kitchen," I would have thought that perfectly fine. I mean I really was skinny, I doubt the scale tipped 120 lbs and I was beginning my ascent to 6' tall. So that day Mrs. Carson endeared herself to me. I told Brian once about his perfect mom but I don't think he understood the warmth I felt in his home.

Some of the kids thought I was pretty smart especially in math and the sciences. I didn't really think that. The logic of math and science just seemed pretty straight forward to me.

Although in school, my friends were the kids who were in similar classes, after school they were completely different. Jim, Rusty, and our new friend Neal Lage began to hang out a lot. The weekends began with Friday night drinking, and then off to the dance at the YMCA on Garfield Street. We began to meet different girls. We soon noticed some girls from Oswego. They would come in after the football games with their cheerleading outfits on and we were pumped. Rusty would talk with Candy Luft and I would talk and dance with Leann Spouts. None of us had cars, so we weren't really in a position to date. But, Friday nights were like dates. We could dance, talk and maybe sneak a kiss.

On Saturday mornings, we would walk the huge block around town in Aurora, down Galena to Broadway, over to Downer Place and then to Stolp Ave and then back to Galena. Round and round we would walk for hours. Leann and her friends would come down from Oswego and we would walk together. I would have walked around town all morning and all afternoon just for the chance to walk 10 minutes with Leann. Back then, Aurora downtown was bustling with some very nice shops. Sencenbaughs, Carson Pirie Scott, Noble Shoes, Benders, and all these stores were anchored by the Paramount Theater. At one point of time there were 3 movie theaters in downtown Aurora, the Paramount, the Tivoli, and the Isle theaters.

Now, the importance of the downtown to me was tantamount. It was close enough from my home where I could easily walk. It was there that I could establish who I was. It is where I began to wear my ten foot scarf wrapped once around my neck, where I wore hats from the 1930's not even being sure if they were male or female hats. Downtown is where my buddies taught me how to put spittle on two pennies and place them in the nickel slot of a pay phone to slow them down so they registered as nickels to make a call. They also showed me how to jam the pay phone so that later you could hit the coin return and get a bunch of change out. They also knew how to open parking meters, but I would never do that.

The YMCA and downtown is also where I met Kathy Porter.

Kathy had straight blonde-brown hair that ran down past her shoulders. She was spunky and really cute. The more I got to know Kathy the more I liked her but with the realization that there could never be any romantic interest. Kathy was straight as an arrow. Not that Leann or Candy weren't the nicest girls in the world, they were. Leann was an officer in her high school class, she was in plays, her grades impeccable. I had no idea why Leann had any interest in me. Maybe I was the wild child she wanted to reform. I used to call Leann every day after school. I loved to hear her voice. Well, even though Kathy Porter was not my girlfriend, she always seemed special. One day she gave me a card in an envelope. I had no idea what this was all about and why she would even give me a card. I opened it. In the card in big letters it said,

God Loves You.
I think about you and I pray for you.
Love Ya,
Kathy

It had such an impact! It was as though I had waited for this letter since second grade where a hole in my heart was first created. I loved this letter Kathy gave me so much I put it in my guitar case and I saved it for years. When I got a little lonely or discouraged I would see it at the bottom of my guitar case and a good feeling would come over me. I never forgot that note, never ever in my life.

Downtown is also where Jim Lautwein and I came down one evening about 1:30 in the morning. We threw full beer bottles as high as we could and watched them pulverize in the middle of the street, right at the corner of Downer Street and Broadway where the old Merchants Bank used to be. Downtown was where much of my socialization took place, both good and bad. It was where I began to find my identity.

Saturday afternoons, Neal and I would often take the train into Chicago from the Aurora Station on South Broadway. From

Chicago's Union Station we would take the elevated train to Wells Street. That's where in the coldest evenings of winter we would walk through Old Town. There were shops there and they cavorted to the hippie crowd. I would save every bit of money I had just so I could buy unusual clothes and shoes. Coach McDougal at West Aurora High School loved my pixie shoes. Well, he at least he commented on them all the time. Neal and I felt very comfortable in Chicago. We would stay in Old Town until the stores shut down. If we couldn't find a place to stay we would go back to Union Station and sleep on a bench until we could board the first train home on Sunday morning. Security didn't want us sleeping there so we would find little cubby holes where we could stay undetected.

I began to meet other kids who were into this new rock scene, kids that also did not answer to their parents. I became friends with Mike Reedy and his pals. We hung out with some of the hippies from Batavia and neighboring cities. I became even more rebellious at home. One night I came home about two in the morning. My mom was sitting in her chair facing the door.

"Where have you been son?" Momma said.

"Don't wait up for me Mom. If you do I just won't come home at night."

I went to my room and fell asleep. I did say that and it pains me so much to admit this. It drives a stake right through my heart to know that I could be that callous. But I was.

My friends and I began to seriously drink and smoke. We would stay out all night whenever possible sleeping in milk trucks, roofs, parks, and fields just so we wouldn't have to go back home. The music of Motown, the Beatles, the Beach Boys, the Animals, and the Rolling Stones were the backdrop of our partying which became wilder and wilder.

CHAPTER 13

Senior Year of High School

After an electrifying summer of embracing this new culture, I was about to begin my senior year. I was truly becoming a rebel. I walked to school the very first day of my senior year as I always did. My knee high boots and long hair would be my signature. It was about a 40 minute walk. I barely made it to the sidewalk outside of the school when a teacher grabbed me and took me straight to the principal's office. I was over 50 feet away from the door and I was already being targeted.

The assistant principal, Mr. Dorsey said, "You can't wear those boots."

I told him, "I have a pair of shoes in my knapsack, I will change them out."

"You can't wear that jacket."

It was a simple shirt jacket. It was purple. It had no writing on it. I couldn't figure this one out.

"As soon as I am assigned a locker, I will take it off and place it in the locker," I replied in a non-belligerent tone.

"Your hair is too long. You are suspended."

Now that hurt. I had to cut my precious hair, my curly flowing hair. Nobody wants to cut their hair and here I was in the dilemma of having to cut my hair or not get back into school. Now my hair wasn't that long, but by the 1966 standards anything over the ear or more than an inch long on the top was too long. Not till later that morning did I find out that Mike Reedy was also suspended and we partied with friends all afternoon.

I got my haircut and went back to school with no coat and no boots. "Your hair is still too long." Mr. Dorsey said. I grimaced at that statement and came to the conclusion that I was not his favorite student. I went home and got another haircut and returned to school the next day.

"You can't have any sideburns. You are suspended." Now, at 16 years old, I had no facial hair and any sideburns only went half way down my ear. I was getting worried that I might never get back into school. But alas, with an almost complete shave of my head they let me back into school. Now those three days of suspension gave me zeroes in my classes and now somehow I would have to get my grades up. It wasn't going to be easy because if I couldn't get my work done in study hall, I sure wasn't going to do much at home.

Chemistry with Mr. Ebeling

I enjoyed most of my classes but I seemed to do especially well in chemistry. My chemistry teacher, Mr. Ebeling, saw something in me. He would banter with me a little during class but he knew how to keep me under control. One day he began to keep me after class and said,

"Dave, you have potential to do a lot of things in life. You need to study hard. You need to reflect on where you want to go and what you want to become."

He would often lecture me in this stern but caring way. He would take me into his small preparation laboratory and sit me down. As he sat next to me he would gaze straight into my eyes and understand the multiple worlds where I lived. I never minded our talks because I knew Mr. Ebeling cared. As we talked, the time would get away from us and I frequently arrived late to my next class. I told Miss Hessling, my sociology teacher, to please talk with Mr. Ebeling and as was keeping me after class. She later came to me and said,

"OK, I have spoken with Mr. Ebeling and he has assured me,

that for good reason, he is keeping you late. I will not hold you accountable, but get here promptly after your discussions."

"Yes, Miss Hessling."

Now Mr. Ebeling had a unique way of encouraging his top students. He would post all the exam grades on the wall next to the door of the classroom. There would be no names associated with the numeric grades except for the 2 or 3 highest grades. There it was,

David V. - 99

Michael L. - 97

Then there was a whole array of lower scores with many D's and F's but no identifying names. There was a small buzz going around as to how the hippie in the mod shirts, crazy shoes and clothes was getting the highest grade in the most dreaded class in high school. I loved every second, every minute, every hour that my name and grade were posted. It made me relevant. My PE teacher, Mr. McDougal, called me "Niño with the pixie shoes" but in chemistry I was the MAN!

It was my senior year and I knew I had to begin thinking about college. No one in my family had gone to college. I had no idea where to apply and what schools to choose. I took my ACTs and I think I did well. I didn't know much about schools other than Aurora College and the new Waubonsee Community College. I saw Drake University on television's "Its Academic" so I applied there. A lot of my classmates were planning on attending the University of Illinois so that sounded good too. But the one thing I knew, I was going to be a chemist and would one day have a Ph.D.

My senior year ended and graduation was quickly approaching. I hadn't thought much about it other than getting my cap and gown. As I readied myself that evening to walk through the ceremony, I realized that no one from my family would be coming. It fit the part. I would be there by myself. Not that this terribly bothered me since I could not remember a single school function of mine that anyone attended since the 4th grade tumbling show with Mr. Hinck at Hermes Elementary.

Jim Lautwein and Rusty Ostreko came to my graduation and that was fine because I knew we were going to seriously party after that. I might not even come home. I wasn't sure anyone really cared. It wasn't long after that, all of my family decided to leave Illinois. My dad had already left for California to start a small restaurant. Mom and Lonnie later took the train to California. They later came back to pick up Aunt Mary. Phil had gotten married and was going into the Marines. I moved into what was my sister Lonnie's apartment on Broadway. When she came back in the middle of the summer, she was steamed at how her apartment looked. She wondered how anyone could get a ketchup stain that was the outline of a hotdog on the kitchen ceiling. Lonnie loved her little brother more than I ever knew and she forgave me, but not without a little tongue lashing which I richly deserved.

CHAPTER 14

The University of Illinois

I had been accepted to the University of Illinois in Champaign-Urbana, Illinois. Lonnie took me midsummer to the U of I for some placement tests. As I was about to return home, the last counselor asked me at which dorm I would be living.

"I will stay wherever I am assigned," I casually responded.

"You mean you didn't apply for student housing?"

"No, was I supposed to?" So, my college journey began with me desperately trying to get housing my freshman year. No one in my family had gone to college before and I had no idea what I was doing. But it worked out. I got a room at a three story independent house called the Grenada Club at Fourth and Chalmers with about a 100 students just like me.

The Campus

The University of Illinois is one of the beautiful Land Grant Universities in the United States. It was founded in 1867. In the middle of the school is a spacious Quad with sidewalks, trees and benches. The two anchors of the Quad were the Illini Union Building on the north side and the Auditorium on the south side. Around the west side of the Quad was Altgeld Hall, the Administration Building, The English Building, Lincoln Hall and Gregory Hall. On the east side of the Quad was Harker Hall, Department of Geology Building, Noyes Laboratory, The Chemistry Annex, Davenport Hall, The Foreign Language Building, and Smith Memorial Hall.

The Quad was the central location of the whole university. Right at the corner of Wright Street and Green Street by Altgeld Hall stood the Alma Mater. I would often gaze at the beautiful sculpture of our University Mother with her welcoming arms. Alma Mater was more than just the school we attended, she was there to watch over us.

The Alma Mater at the University of Illinois

The Quad was also where students studied under the trees on beautiful fall days while kites and Frisbees graced the air. It is where the two most important buildings for me were located, Noyes

Laboratory and The Chemistry Annex. Eleven Nobel Laureates in chemistry had graced these halls of which I would soon attend. North of the Quad were the engineering buildings, northeast was the physics building, and to the east the New Krannert Center was being built. It was a sprawling growing university.

My freshman and sophomore years were organized on two principles. My program was to first go to class and study hard from Sunday afternoon till Friday afternoon, then second, party hard from Friday night till Sunday noon. I was never really organized in high school but somehow I transformed into a study jock as soon as I got to college. Maybe I realized that I was truly on my own. Every day I would set up a study schedule for the evening. I even scheduled my breaks. It would look something like this.

6:00-6:30	Eat Dinner
6:30-7:30	Calculus
7:30-8:30	Physics
8:30-8:45	Take a break
8:45-10:00	Chemistry
10:00-11:00	German
11:00-11:30	Wrap up any loose assignments
11:30-12:00	Crash for the evening

Without fail, I would make a daily schedule and follow it. Now on the weekends, it was often over to the Little Brown Jug. We would listen to bands and buy pitchers of beer. We would sometimes make it over to Kams but I never seemed to really like it there. Sometimes, we would chip in and bring kegs of beer into our Independent House.

When I wanted to go home and be with old friends, I would hitchhike the 129 miles to Aurora. Every holiday, Thanksgiving, Christmas, Semester Break, Spring Break, I would have to hitchhike home as I had no ride, or means to get home. I would put my thumb out and hope to get a ride. And then I would hitchhike back to school. I didn't mind, it was a way of life to me. I met many different types of people some of whom offered me things I cannot describe in this book.

I made the Dean's list every semester. It wasn't long before I thought to myself, 'if I took extra classes I could graduate in 3½ years.' So in my second semester sophomore year I took Organic Chemistry, Physical Chemistry, Physical Chemistry Lab, Physics, German, Differential Equations and Orthogonal Functions, and Square Dancing. Needless to say, I did not enjoy a single minute of that semester and determined that only an idiot would voluntarily subject himself to that type of torture. Somehow I managed to still make the Dean's list but not without paying the deep price of utter exhaustion. I said to myself, I like school. Why am I killing myself?

CHAPTER 15

Junior Year of College 1969-1970

The Selective Service Lottery

My junior year began with me living in a house on First Street with about 9 other guys. We rented it for about 50 dollars a month a piece. We had no food service so we just cooked our own meals. I started a meal job at the chemical fraternity across campus. We set up or cleaned up lunch and dinner, and earned a meal made by the biggest Elvis fan this side of the Mississippi, our cook Mabel. I was taking Advanced Calculus, Physical Chemistry/Thermodynamics, Inorganic Chemistry, Physics, and an elective.

The first semester of my Junior Year was most memorable. The Vietnam War was raging and men were coming home in body bags and wheel chairs. The news on TV was not good as it became apparent that they needed more men to fight. The draft was being reinstituted and an equitable means of inducting men into military service was devised. On my 20th birthday was the selective service lottery. The lottery determined the order which you would be called to serve in the armed forces when you became 18 or lost your deferment. So, 366 plastic balls each with a day of the calendar written on them were placed in a big glass container. And one by one the plastic balls were drawn to determine the order you were drafted into the military in the year your deferment ended.

So, 10 young men in our room, 20,000 young men on our campus, and millions of young men across the United States were all glued to their television or radio to find out the fate of their lives.

The drawing began with the first blue ball with the date September 14. It seemed as though we all screamed simultaneously,

"You're dead, dudes."

Nobody in our group of 10 was going to be drafted, not yet. As the evening began, the emotional roller coaster was incomprehensible. The only thing I could somehow compare to this night was when I watched the Ten Commandments with Charlton Heston as Moses. In the depth of this night, December 1, 1969, an eerie fog permeated every home in America in the form of the Angel of Death. Here, it would surely not devour the first born, but in an instant it marked the birthdays of the first students to be drafted upon loss of their deferments.

But, how could anyone be so unlucky for their birth date to be drawn first? From the day they were born, they cherished that date, the parties, the love, the gatherings associated with that day. But tonight that date, September 14, was toxic, the unluckiest number ever born. And just as in the movie, the wailing began.

Each of us waited on pins and needles for the number associated with our birthdays to be called. The first hour passed and we had reached 100 balls pulled. My birthday had not been called. Up to 125 and I had not been called.

And the 129th ball drawn, December 1.

"This can't be," I groaned from the depths of my soul. "I am going to Vietnam."

That night there was a lot of drinking and smoking marijuana. For those with the low numbers, the abject stunning reality that they would be drafted into the armed services beat them into utter depression, and those with the highest numbers with the certainty that they would never be coerced into the army lifted them into the highest level of exultation. But for those of us in the middle, especially the lower middle, like myself, the uncertainty and the painful wait had just begun on this day on my birthday.

The draft began almost immediately. So for those unlucky souls born in the years 1944-1950 who had no school or health deferment, they were being called to report for their physicals and then induction. Merry Christmas 1969 and Happy New Year 1970.

We all left campus for Christmas Break, and then returned for exams in January. After semester break, there was a new atmosphere on campus. The television reports of US deaths sunk deeper into our psyche. For 1969, 11,780 American men died in Vietnam, 32 men every day. The real question was, what choice did I have? What course of action could I or should I take? These questions undoubtedly resonated in each student at every university in America.

The Anti-War Movement Races into Full Swing

In the midst of these events crept an uneasiness on campus. The Walrus and The Geek, underground newspapers, kept us informed on rallies, and the response and activities of the University. The major issues beyond the Vietnam War were the establishment of University relationships with companies that were benefactors of the War such as General Electric (GE) and Dow Chemical. When their corporate recruiters came, so did the disruptions. Other issues included the Illiac IV, a supercomputer being developed for military use, and the banning of William Kunstler, attorney for the Chicago 7. The Chicago 7 were the men charged with conspiracy to incite riots during the 1968 Democratic Convention. For me, the issue was the Vietnam War and our participation.

In October, the first large demonstrations began with over 9,000 people on the Quad. Speakers ranted on injustices on the front steps of the Auditorium. As I looked around at the sea of people, I felt immersed, lost in the dialogue of a movie. The demonstration ended without any major incidents but it forebode the coming waves of student unrest.

The March Riots

The beginning of March came and so did the strife. GE was recruiting and in protest, students occupied the Engineering Building on the north side of Campus. The students left the engineering building and headed towards Campus town on Green Street. I had coaxed Sully, one of my roommates, to join me that day. We stayed together as long as possible but when the chaos began, I would not see him till much later that night.

About 500-1000 students gathered and began marching west from the corner of Green and Wright Street where the Alma Mater stood. I had assembled with other students a block down at Sixth and Green Street. As the students began their surge toward us, you could hear echoes of shattered glass all along Campus Town. Like locusts devouring a field, some of the students were insatiable in their destructive desires. Student marshals bellowed from their bull horns,

"Don't destroy property. Don't destroy property."

It helped for a moment but then the crescendo of violence re-erupted. The students continued down Green Street toward Sixth Street where a group of about 25-35 state and local policemen had strategically positioned themselves. There would be a major confrontation, a collision of two worlds. Side by side the police stood, close enough to interlock arms if they chose. With their helmets and face shields in place, they led with their left foot and then thrust a long baton straight forward into the bodies of students and stepped ahead. Left foot, thrust, step ahead. It was like a Roman Legion crushing an unarmed people with the sole prize of victory. As they moved forward in their phalanx formation, student after student fell to the ground, with some students holding their heads and others clasping their abdomens.

Unknown to the police at this time was that as they progressed down the middle of Green Street toward Wright Street, a second set of students from Sixth Street where I stood, began following closely behind them totally closing off any rear escape route for the police. All during this time objects continued to be hurled at the police and at the stores along Green Street. When the police realized their potentially catastrophic error, they stopped and began to backtrack to where I was, at the corner of Sixth and Green.

Students had now blocked the police in at the intersection of Sixth and Green. There were hundreds of students blocking each direction, to the North, to the South, to the West, and to the East where the angriest students who had taken the severe beat down stood. Everything I knew about peace and civility was about to end as the policemen were cornered in on all sides at the intersection of Sixth and Green. As the police retreated into a defensive position with their shields, a barrage of projectiles continued to be directed squarely into their midst.

"Do not throw objects at the Police. We don't want to hurt them," blasted the student bull horns. "We are going to let them leave through the north side of Sixth Street. Stand back! We are letting them out!"

The students began to disperse on the north side of Sixth Street with police officers in full retreat. As the police abandoned their position, students continued to launch debris at the officers. It was full scale chaos.

"Sully," I said, "We got to get out of here now."

And even though I said this, I felt compelled to stay and watch the most unimaginable event to occur. Coming up from north side of Sixth Street where the police had just retreated were 3 armored Jeeps, each with barbed wire type fencing secured to the front bumper. I gasped. It became evident that they were going to clear these streets by force. All I could think was, 'tonight somebody is going to die.'

A hush, then the yelling and screaming got louder as the 3 Jeeps turned left onto Green Street in the direction of the Illini Union. Side by side the Jeeps slowly proceeded forward taunting any student to stand in the way. As the students retreated, it became obvious that the police had the upper hand and we had no way to withstand this show of force. The Jeeps made their way to the Alma Mater where she stood so bravely with her loving outstretched arms.

As we broke for the evening, the blood on student's faces and shirts was a clear indication of what was yet to come. I am neither certain how many students were arrested, nor how many windows were broken but I know the damage was devastating to the store owners. In all the confusion Sully and I again became separated. We met back at home and we told our roommates what we had seen. Some had been there, too.

We were being told through underground newspapers to be prepared for the next demonstration. We were to wrap newspapers around our arms to protect ourselves against the force of clubs and to bring hankies to cover our mouths and faces in case of tear gas. Most of the marches during the week were at night and soon they began again. About 4500 students marched to President Henry's mansion and about 2,000 students to the Armory where the ROTC was based. The marchers turned to Campus Town and resumed the ravaging of windows. There was a 10:30 pm curfew and most of us didn't want to get arrested. We had made our point and retreated. Tomorrow would be another day.

By the next day, the Governor ordered 700 national guardsmen to the U of I. They surrounded the campus armed with weapons. The violence subsided during the next few weeks. By the time GE left the campus, more than $20,000 damage had been done to campus buildings.

The Week of Chaos
Monday, May 4, 1970

It had been very quiet on campus throughout the month of April. Anti-war rhetoric continued but students were intent on finishing their studies and taking exams. Then it happened, a news bulletin. Four students shot dead by National Guard at Kent State University in Ohio. Three of the students were not even involved in the demonstrations and only one might have had radical tendencies.

Sandy Scheuer, 20 years young, of Youngstown, Ohio. Shot in the neck and killed. She had been searching for her lost dog.

William Schroeder, 19 years young, of Lorain, Ohio. He was an ROTC member and was only an observer.

Allison Krause, 19 years young, of Pittsburg, PA. She and her boyfriend had simply been walking to class.

Jeffrey Glenn Miller, 20 years young, of Plainview NY. He may have been there to protest but it was not confirmed as he was not directly involved with any militants.

Tuesday, May 5, 1970
Organizers were making a set of demands that the University simply could not agree to.

Termination of US involvement into Cambodia

Freedom of All Political Prisoners

Termination of Repression of the Black Panthers

Impeachment of President Nixon

End of University complicity with the Military

There was now a call for a strike to force the University to meet their demands. Tensions were beginning to mount. The realization for many students was at year end their deferment would end and they were going to Vietnam. This was their last gasp. I still had another year of student deferment but I was just as upset by the injustices being thwarted upon me.

Wednesday May 6, 1970
It wasn't just another day. It was a clear sunny Spring day where temperatures climbed into the high 70s. It was the type of day that you simply wished you were at the beach sipping a frozen margarita. It was midday and I had just ended a class in the Physics Building on Green Street. I began my westward trek back to my apartment on First Street when I noticed a commotion in front of the Illini Union Building. A number of students, 50-100, had sat down in the circle drive stopping all vehicular traffic. The police in riot gear with 3½ foot billy clubs had arrived and the students were chanting,

"No More War. Shut the University down."

The group seemed somewhat subdued perhaps because of its

small size and the time of day. I recognized Professor Michael Parenti sitting near the front of the crowd on the left side of the circle drive as you faced the Illini Union. Dr. Parenti was an activist professor who had gained some notoriety. I did not personally know him, but he was easily identifiable not only to me but also to the police. No doubt he was a target. Now I don't care what the newspapers wrote about that day or what anyone said. The activists were settled in their demeanor and were not belligerent. I had not yet decided whether to participate and sit down with them when,

"Smack!" whipped a baton across the top of Professor Michael Parenti's head. The policeman who struck him hovered over him like a drill sergeant on the first day of boot camp. Nobody moved. Professor Parenti's eyes glazed as he was stunned from the ferocity of the blow that bobbed his head. None of the students moved in apparent shock of the callous violence. I stood paralyzed by the thunder created by the blow crashing onto Michael Parenti's head. The professor never raised his hand, never raised a fist. He just sat there with blood running over his eye and down his face, his head split open like a watermelon on the 4th of July. The police picked him up, dragged him to the police van and began to disperse the remaining students, clubbing whomever they pleased. Those that resisted were arrested. There would be a price to pay as news spread throughout the campus. There was going to be trouble, yeah a lot of trouble!

It was relatively quiet that night even though over 4,000 had gathered in a protest rally. An 8 pm curfew had been imposed and organizers had not yet decided what to do. Over 2,000 National Guardsmen were now at the University fully armed and ready to be employed. There were some reports of skirmishes but I was not a part of it, nor did I see it.

Thursday May 7, 1970
Non-violent demonstrations occurred throughout the day. By evening 10,000 students, 1/3 of the student body was on the Quad

peacefully protesting. I could only think about having a camera to film the immensity of the surreal mass of humanity. About 900 guardsman stood by outside the Quad. They had been issued live ammunition according to reports. They had even brought a flame thrower. Were they going to torch students? Really?

Friday May 8, 1970

Midday, I joined the group going to Central Receiving and the Physical Plant Services Building. These buildings were located on the Southwest Side of Campus directly west of Memorial Stadium. Between the Stadium and the Services building was a large field, Stadium Terrace Play Field, about the size of 6 city blocks. This was where we first gathered and planned.

We then crossed the street and headed towards Central Receiving and the Physical Plant. Our strategy was to disrupt all services to the University. As we began to block trucks from entering and leaving, the police began to arrive in large numbers, equipped with helmets, batons, and guns. There was an air of both fear and excitement. As our protest line disintegrated, several policemen began to chase us into Stadium Terrace Play Field. Directly behind me was a policeman waving a billy club chasing a group of students but then he seemed to focus on me. As I zagged left, the policemen zagged left. As I zagged right, he zagged right. I wasn't waving a billy club. I didn't have a heavy belt with a walky-talky, handcuffs, and a gun. I didn't have a helmet. I just had me.

Something was happening here that was explosive. The moment seemed to stretch out as seconds appeared to be minutes, and minutes into hours. Every step I took symbolized the battle lines that were drawn. Every breath was an expression of my need to declare my freedom. In this visual optic, I could see the clouds billowing in a bright blue sky over Stadium Terrace Play Field and I wasn't afraid. And as this surreal scene was burning in slow motion in my mind, the reality dawned that the policeman chasing me was closing in on me.

But I came from a family of runners. I ran from my mom. I ran from my dad. I ran from Old Man Schott. I ran from that bus driver and I ran from the police. A dozen cops weren't going to catch me that day, not ever. No way!

With my adrenaline running full force through my veins, I began to distance myself from that cop. As he tired, I could see him slow down and then a vicious,

"Thud."

Another student smacked that cop with a bat on the back of his calf and he went down. He fell down in that grass grimacing in pain, clutching the back of his leg. I would have stopped to help that cop but not now, not with his fellow officers racing to assist him. I never wanted to hurt anyone. I just wanted to be the class clown. They just didn't need any in Vietnam.

Saturday May 9, 1970

Early in the afternoon, students gathered by the Alma Mater, between Altgeld Hall and the Illini Union building. We would continue to chant slogans on ending the war and the oppression of students. Occasionally a group of students would go into the intersection of Wright and Green Street and stop traffic, but they quickly dispersed before any police escalation took place.

I was getting tired and thirsty as this little demonstration continued for hours. I went in to the Quad just south of the Illini Union building and decided to rest for a moment. The atmosphere was peaceful with some students studying and others throwing Frisbees. But, there was something in the air like when a deer first catches the scent of a wolf. I got up and I told my friends.

"Let's go. We got to move. NOW!"

We headed down the Quad past the administration building and barely past the English building and my intuition proved true. About 10 police officers sprinted into the Quad from Wright Street between the English Building and Lincoln Hall. They were yelling and waving their batons forcing any and all students into the center of the Quad. I moved quickly to hug the inside hedges of the English Building. As the officers raced past me, I saw it. There were officers from between each building on the Quad, billy clubs in hand, barking and prodding at students like cattle on the Abilene trail. Over 100 students were pushed into a small circle right there in the middle of the Quad and ordered to sit down. Then a series of buses were driven into the Quad next to the students where they were ordered onto the buses. How could they indiscriminately arrest all these students? I was sure that the majority of them were not involved in anything but relaxing on the Quad. The protests were occurring outside the Quad. I should have been on that bus. I was guiltier than most that sat peering out those bus windows at a University that had betrayed them. When those buses left there was no one left on the Quad. I could only wonder what would happen next.

Then word came that they were taken to the Football Stadium to be processed and arrested. Among those arrested were a reporter from the Daily Illini, a University TV newsman, a botanist studying plants and trees in the Quad, and a whole host of students I knew were not involved in any way. Rallies of over 6,000 students followed but they were without the violence of earlier demonstrations.

CHAPTER 16

Summer 1970

By the end of my Junior Year, things began to simmer down on the anti-war front. Exams had to be taken, dorms emptied, and summer plans established. I applied and got a job at Argonne National Laboratories in Lemont, Illinois. It did seem ironic to be fiercely protesting the war and the government, and the next month making a salary at one of the largest government laboratories. Argonne was initially formed to continue Enrico Fermi's work on the Manhattan Project of nuclear bombs and reactors.

I worked in Building 202, Medical and Biological Research, for Dr. Herb Kubitschek. Dr. Kubitschek had worked for Enrico Fermi at the University of Chicago as they first harnessed nuclear energy. It was a great summer culminating in my first paper published, "Efficiency of Thymidine Incorporation in Escherichia coli B/r as a Function of Growth Rate" (Journal of Bacteriology) with the authors H.E. Kubitschek, D. Valdez and M.L. Freedman.

Dave in his Hippie Years

CHAPTER 17

Senior Year at Illinois 1970-1971

Summer passed quickly. I went to several rock concerts and became somewhat accustomed to recreational drug use. I was careful not to exceed my limits. It was time to begin thinking about school again. I had classes to schedule and a new apartment to move my belongings. By this time, I had met most of my liberal arts requirements with the exception of humanities. I really didn't even know what humanities were. I guessed it had very little to do with chemistry and the sciences. But, it was looming before me; I couldn't graduate without two semesters of humanities.

Having little desire to study in an area of no interest to me, I debated what class on human existence could I take that would be the easiest. And there it was in the course offerings, the Old Testament and New Testament as literature. I thought, OK, I have never read the Bible. Well I tried once and quit after two pages into Genesis. And then I thought "how hard could this class really be?" So, mixed in with hard core sciences and math, I was going to study the Bible. Little did I know what a profound effect these classes would have on me.

I moved in into a three person apartment with Sully and Ed. They both had lived with me last year. Sully was well liked by everyone. Ed was a brilliant nerd type civil engineer. One of his friends told me he was number one in his civil engineering class. I had no reason to doubt that.

Across the hall from me in an identical apartment lived Rod Gerig, Ray Haliski, and Bob Cahill. I was especially close with Rod and Ray even more so than my own roommates. We talked about a lot of things but foremost on our minds was our lottery number and our majors. There was no doubt that the Spring of 1970 left me radicalized and certainly more apt to drink and party. It surely didn't help to be constantly reminded in every newscast how many Americans died in Vietnam that day. As for me, I knew I would be drafted and Vietnam bound which undoubtedly in my mind meant death or disfiguration. I had a whole year to consider going to Canada or to devise a plan to avoid the draft. I did neither.

I began to apply to Graduate Schools where I would obtain a Ph.D. in chemistry. It was a little confusing because I knew my deferment would end next June. But what was I supposed to do? Stop living? Forgo the most important event, the dream that I had carried since high school? So, I began to consider schools: Michigan – nope, Boston College – no way, Maryland - no chance. I was going to California where every young man could reach his dreams or so I thought. I applied to Berkeley, Stanford, UCLA and UCSB. I applied to the University of California Santa Barbara for one reason alone. On February 25, 1970 during the anti-war riots, the students burned down the Bank of America building. Nothing more, nothing less. Berkeley, Stanford and UCLA were my choices but UCSB was my fall back.

My senior year of college began with so much on my mind. But there was also the beautiful aspect of college that I so loved. In the beginning of each school year when the evening temperatures are perfect, there is an aura of something new, innocent and great. The bands begin playing outdoors and students mingle as they meet new friends and renew old acquaintances. I especially loved the first week before classes because there were no worries about class work and exams.

It was early in the evening on a moonlit September night and I was headed down Fourth Street towards the University Residence Halls. I could hear a band playing loud music and all the students were laughing and singing. There was ornamental lighting that hung from tree to tree that just begged for kids to believe in a better life. Out of the corner of my eye, I saw Kathy Porter and she saw me.

"Dave," she shrieked.

"Kathy," I yelled. "I didn't know you were coming to school here. Why didn't you say something?"

"I don't know, but I am so glad I found you," and she hugged and clung to me for a moment as though she had been lost and I had found her. Her eyes told me that she was nervous about this new experience.

I had never quite realized the age difference before, I was a senior and she was a freshman. We sat down and talked about all our old friends and what classes we were taking. I told her about the riots last year and how so many things had happened.

"I would never have let you do that Dave." I could only notice that Kathy was even more beautiful than before. Her light brown almost blonde hair was so straight, it totally contrasted my wavy black Afro.

"I would have never let you come with me Kathy." We laughed, hugged, and left it at that.

Kathy came over to my apartment where my roommates were having a small party. We had music and some dancing. Ed, my roommate, asked Kathy to dance. She, being the consummate young lady, said yes. I could see Eddie's demeanor and eyes as he danced with probably the most beautiful woman he had ever chanced upon.

As I walked Kathy home, I asked,

"Do you have a phone number so I can call you?"

"Sure Dave, and let me have yours."

We began to meet a few times at the Illini Union cafeteria. We talked mostly about classes, politics, and the war. God would come up and then I would mostly listen. We never argued about anything. Kathy knew I was a rebellious kid. She knew I would not bring her into my world. I stopped seeing her just because of all the pressures of school. In all our conversations I never told her that I still had the card that she gave me years ago. It was in the bottom of my guitar case. It's hard to understand that our friendship was so unique and now we would not talk again until the day she told me she was leaving school for good and going back home to Oswego, Illinois.

The Violence Begins Again

It wasn't long before the heightened awareness of the atrocities in Vietnam once again would motivate students to riot. Not to the intensity of the Spring of 1970, but still a contingent of students was intent on making a statement in hopes of stopping the war. It was late Fall that we began again. The corner of Wright and Green Street by the Alma Mater seemed to be a place where the unrest often began. There she was, our Alma Mater standing 13 feet tall. Her outstretched hands embodied peace, yet we were embroiled in a cause and a fight that did not seem to have an ending.

"Three, Four, Stop the War."

"Three, Four, Stop the War."

As the number of protesting students began to climb, so did the police presence. I was with Emma, a friend I had met. She had short brown hair and was a science major like me. During the protests I preferred to be linked to someone who could help in a time of need, be a look out for your blind side. As more policemen arrived, we retreated past Altgeld Hall towards the Quad. It was a dark evening and it seemed like students were silhouettes in the shadows around me, yelling and racing in different directions. As the larger group passed Altgeld Hall, then the Henry Administration building, the reverberations of smashed windows hammered down the Quad. The police raced in to try to squelch the violence. As the students scattered, I looked for Emma in each direction. There she was 30 feet in front of me.

"Emma," I shouted. "Follow me!"

"Where we going?" she pleaded as the turmoil escalated and the police were beginning to arrest students.

"Shut up, just come with me!" I took her hand and we raced to the side of Noyes Laboratory on the northeast side of the Quad.

I had been given a key to the building since much of my senior research was done outside of normal hours. Quickly I inserted the key, opened the door, entered and slammed it shut behind us. I took Emma downstairs and through an underground tunnel to Adams laboratory outside the Quad. I held Emma by the shoulders for a few minutes to calm her and then we went back out onto the street on Matthews Avenue outside of the Quad. We tried to look and see what remained of the demonstration but we couldn't go back into the Quad. Not now. We went and had a beer and talked about the evening and speculated what the activists might be planning next.

Within a few days, there was going to be a march between the Illini Union Building and the Urbana County Courthouse. Over the last few days a number of students had been arrested and we wanted to know where they were being detained. There were about 200 of us who started at the Illini Union. It seemed like such a paltry number. No doubt, the movement was slowly dying. Much of the passion was gone. Nevertheless, we began our trek concerning ourselves only with the cause. The courthouse was about 12 blocks directly east of the Union right on Green Street. As we approached the Urbana Courthouse, we began chanting in endless fashion,

"Free the Political Prisoners"

"Free the Political Prisoners"

The police were expecting us. All of the entrances were barricaded and the police stood shoulder to shoulder ensuring that we did not even get onto the sidewalks. We continued our chants for at least an hour marching around the building hurling insults and demands. The police were videotaping the entire demonstration in hopes of identifying who they surely considered the hard core activists. After about two exhaustive hours, we began marching back to the Union where we would discuss the next steps. As I walked to the Union with my fellow students around me, the events of the day began to weigh heavily on me. I thought to myself,

"I don't even know who is in jail. What exactly am I doing here?"

It struck me like lightning, like a blue bolt in a summer thunderstorm,

"I don't even know who is in jail and I am not sure anyone else does."

There I was walking down the middle of Green Street with students whose names I didn't even know. I was yelling and screaming about social injustice creating a spectacle to a whole town. I had never really thought it through. I knew there were many ugly things going on in this world, but I had no idea who was incarcerated, nor the real reason. I had to be smarter than that.

We dispersed as we approached the Illini Union but there were no goodbyes to my fellow protesters. There were no affirmations that we had done well, or we even did the right thing. All I knew was that a blue bolt struck a nerve in me and I twitched. I knew something had happened that turned my head. I had to get a clearer understanding of who I was and what I was doing. And when the rain and thunder cleared in my mind, I knew I would never participate in another anti-war rally.

CHAPTER 18

The Meetings

There seemed to be so much indecision and questioning going on in my life. It was my last semester. As I began to take my New Testament class, I immediately felt the professor's antagonism toward Christianity. As he disparaged God, I felt no motivation to defend God although several students did. I could tell they were offended. They would raise their hands and question the professor. I remained silent nary a word on my lips. Why would I defend Christianity anyway? And why argue with a fool, I thought. I just had to pass this class and be done with it.

About this time my friends with lower lottery numbers were getting notices to report for their selective service physicals in anticipation of their deferment ending at graduation. I had not received my notice yet but I purposed to do something. I decided to lose weight to a level that no one could possibly consider me draftable material. I was always skinny. I was 6'2" tall and about 140 lbs. I began my slow fast only minimally eating when needed.

Just a Question

On a warm Spring Day, I was sitting on the steps of the Union building at the Quad reading a book about St.Paul for my New Testament class when a stranger approached me. He sat next to me and looked at the book I was reading.

"What are you reading?" he asked, fully aware of what I was reading. Did I look like some kind of DooFuss?

"I am reading a book about the Apostle Paul for my humanities

81

class," I said barely looking up to acknowledge him. He was neatly dressed with a button down collar shirt and a pair of khakis. There are different types of people at every large university and you quickly can sum up with whom you would engage in conversation or activity. He was not one.

"Have you read any of the books in the Bible that Paul wrote?" he inquired.

I had hoped that he would quickly leave but I knew I was squarely locked into a conversation that clearly had me on the defensive. Here I am a senior in college soon to be graduating from one of the finest schools in chemistry and this guy is asking me if I know any of the books that Paul wrote. Now who comes and asks a curly haired, skinny kid with bell bottom pants and a torn t-shirt on a sunny afternoon this kind of question? And I so struggled with the answer hoping to sound profound,

"Galatians, Ephesians," and I felt somewhat relieved at my answer. Now if this guy would just leave.

"That's great!" he says. "Would you like to get together and discuss what Paul wrote?" Everything inside me said NO! He doesn't look like me. He doesn't act like me. His hair is so short that I can't tell what color it is. He is probably a Republican and goes to some repressive church.

"We could meet at the YWCA for some coffee."

And for some reason as I was saying no in my mind when, "Yeah, we could do that," blurted out of my mouth.

"Ok, how about Tuesday at 10:00 and by the way my name is Mike."

"I'm Dave. See you then." And I wondered the rest of the day just what I had done and whether I would go.

In my humanities class the rant of the professor continued, "Now Paul has an unstable personality evidenced by the radical transformation from a persecutor of the church to a follower."

I thought that was the Bible story. I didn't take a lot of time to think about this but I was pretty much convinced that the instructor was simply annoyed at the New Testament narrative. I mean couldn't a person change like Paul. It was in the Bible. Although I had no Bible or church training, I had seen enough Christian movies on TV to get an idea of the character of Jesus. As for me, I came from a pretty tame family life or so I thought, and I changed into an anti-war demonstrator and was willing to sacrifice for it. But then again, was I really willing to sacrifice for it? I mean all the peace and love that hippies ascribed to just wasn't so. They would steal from you in an instant for drugs and leave you cold. But, I certainly wasn't ascribing to a government that would send me to die in Vietnam for a cause I did not understand.

By this time my roommate, Sully, had left school. First it was Kathy and now Sully. I don't know what happened to him and no one was talking. One weekend he was just gone. It is really hard to see your friends leave during the school year. It is as though we all are sojourners passing through a tortuous journey of classes, relationships, parties, and foremost of all, decisions. All of our lives we have been nestled in our homes by parents and all of a sudden, we now must make our own paths for better or worse. Some of us had inclinations toward the worse.

Ed and I were roommates and that's about the depth of our relationship. It was a matter of convenience. I spent more time with Rod and Ray from across the hall. Both were good friends but I felt more comfortable with Rod. He liked good music and played some guitar. I would see Rod reading his Bible and Ray had a Bible in his room but I never asked questions about it.

At the YWCA

I managed to make it over to the YWCA. After a few informalities such as getting coffee and talking about the weather, Mike began the conversation,

"Do you believe God exists and wants to be part of your life?" I sat back stunned at how abrupt that question came. It didn't take me long to answer.

"I have never really considered that to be a relevant question.

I mean, look what is going on in this world today. Do you think a loving God is in charge of this wreck? With all the craziness tearing us apart, do you really think he needs to be spending any time on me? Now, think about this Mike, all these people getting killed in Vietnam, Cold War in Eastern Europe, China killing their own people, and now God wants to be part of my life. Isn't that a little disingenuous on your part?"

I had never spoken to anyone about religion before. Nobody really asked and I really had very little to say on the topic. But I felt good about what I said. How could anyone answer all of my questions? As I reflected on my words I realized that maybe I had just acknowledged the existence of a God, just not a God to whom I could relate.

"I have felt that way too, at times," Mike said. "But I have come to recognize that the evil in this world is a result of man stepping away from God."

I replied, "And what about the people of the world who never heard about Jesus? Were they stepping away from God? Or maybe God just stepped away from them." I think I was talking more than Mike and I wasn't getting a lot out of our conversation. It seemed too circuitous and I knew I was being cynical. Everything he said, I could refute or ask another question. My only thought now was, I want to escape and walk away. And if he asks me to meet him again I will simply say "no" and be on my way.

"I really enjoyed this time together. How about if we meet again next week, same time?"

And as the word "no" formed on my lips, I said, "OK, I will be here." Something was drawing me to this young man. Was it his sincerity or his friendliness? I just didn't know but I had said yes when I wanted to say no.

I had now lost about 5 lbs and I was down to 135 lbs. I kept on dieting only eating small amounts to condition my stomach for smaller and smaller portions. I just knew that I would be getting that dreaded letter to report for my draft physical. Instead I received a letter from the University of California, Santa Barbara. I had been accepted into their graduate school with an assistantship to help defray costs. I was excited to receive my first letter. I was going to be teaching undergraduates in laboratory sessions or in classes bridged to classroom instruction. Santa Barbara is located about 95 miles north of Los Angeles. I promptly accepted the offer despite that the draft looming over me might prevent me from ever attending UCSB.

I was well into my final semester at Illinois and classes now seemed to take precedence over everything. I was going to graduate soon and I had to make sure I completed each and every requirement.

Mike Brings a Friend

I met with Mike two more times. This last time he brought a friend. I could only think that I was trapped and I would not meet again with him after this bushwhacking. Even though I did not know how I felt about the topic of God, I didn't want to talk to two people about the Bible, Jesus, and the whatever.

Mike began, "This is Jim. He is a friend of mine from Campus Crusade for Christ."

I said to myself, I now have two guys from Campus Crusade for Christ that are going to interrogate me. I should tell them I have been crusading all my life; inform them on the issues and what is important in life. Maybe I should tell them that they should be out protesting the war with me. People are getting killed everywhere, Americans, Vietnamese, Chinese. Maybe I should tell them …

"Mike has mentioned that you are interested in spiritual things," Jim said.

"Well, yes and no." I stammered. "We have talked and it's been interesting."

Out of the cold blue comes, "Have you ever asked Jesus into your heart?"

Now I am thinking, this guy has only been here 10 minutes and he is trying to dissect me like a frog in a high school biology class.

Jim continued, "I brought this booklet. It's called the Four Spiritual Laws. Do you think we could go over it together?"

And so we started reading this little bitty booklet that Jim brought with him that day. Together we read that God loves me and has a wonderful plan for my life. We are all sinful and separated from God. Jesus died on the cross and spilled his blood as our provision for sin. And then we got to step 4. You must individually accept Jesus Christ into your life. Then, they read John 3:16,

For God so loved the world, that He gave his one and only Son, that whoever believes in Him shall not perish but have eternal life.

With Jim and Mike both fixated on me, I didn't know what to say. Jim broke the silence,

"Would you like to accept Jesus into your life?" Then Jim said, "You can follow after me or read the prayer from the booklet."

Deep within my soul I felt a longing, a need for completion. I had felt a separation, a loneliness all my life. I don't know why but I read the sinner's prayer. I closed my eyes and said to myself,

"Dear Lord, I am a sinner and I know I am separated from you. You died for me. Please come into my life." I kept repeating this prayer, not 1 time, not 2 times, not 3 times, nor 4. And each time I said this prayer I kept feeling the reality of God sink a little deeper into my soul like a pile driver through my hardened heart. I was knocking on heaven's door.

I sat there with my head in hands. It seemed like eternity but each time I repeated the need for God in my life, I felt the caring hand of God. There was not a single concern I had as to what my two guests thought was going on as the silence stretched on. I didn't care about anything other than trying to embrace the One who embraced me now. Still not sure of what exactly happened, I got up from my chair, thanked them, and I never saw them again.

I walked out of the YWCA with a sense of astonishment and bewilderment. I began to skip to my next class across Wright Street, through the Quad and to the chemistry building. I am not sure I had ever seen someone in college who skipped to class, but there I was without a care in the world. The feeling of utter contentment overwhelmed me.

I was still puzzled as I went to bed that night. I lay thinking about the day's events. Had God come into my life? Had God really forgiven me of all my sins by dying on the cross? Is that even possible? I thought of Kathy Porter and how years ago I tucked in my guitar case that note she gave me about God. There it lay hidden to all but me. Had she been praying for me? Was it the anxiety and uncertainties of military service and the anti-war movement weighing heavily in my feelings of desperation? How did it happen that I decided to take the Old Testament and New Testament classes? As I studied the Gospels and the Epistles for my class, they all seemed to have deeper meaning than a collection of stories. And Mike from Campus Crusade, was that just a chance meeting? Could this have been a tapestry that God had woven just for me? I didn't have an answer to any of this. I just wanted to know if this was real. I had been reading the Gospels for my class and found in Matthew,

Knock and the door will be opened to you. Matthew 7.7 NIV

But I wasn't sure if I was knocking. But, I must have.

CHAPTER 19

Tear from the Eye of God

I continued to party hard during the weekends. Sometimes we would have so many kids in our apartment that we would have to sit on the floor with our legs crossed. We would talk about the war, classes, relationships, just about anything. The beer and the smoking flowed heavily at these parties. And before I even realized it, I began confiding in those around me in the midst of my debauchery,

"I asked Jesus to come in to my life and He changed me. I asked Him to forgive me of all my sins and He did. I can't explain it all but something happened in my life."

And so I would often retell my story to mostly disbelieving friends who scoffed. But not Ray and Rod, I would talk to them late in the night. They wanted to hear more of exactly what had happened to me. I had not yet gone to church, never been to a Bible study. I had not even considered whether I was doing right or wrong at these parties and that it might conflict with my new found life. I only knew I couldn't contain myself from telling my story.

One evening I spoke with my friend Bill from Dwight, Illinois. He had lived with me at the Grenada Club and in the group house on First Street. I shared with him my story as it now grew within my soul. In desperation to shut me up he said,

"Where is God now? Is He on your right? Over there, maybe He is on your left? Don't give me this God business cause it isn't real and you know it!"

I knew there was no need to be argumentative with Bill. He was my friend and I had been exactly where he is. I knew his story and he knew mine. And mine had changed big time. No one could deny that. I felt a tear come to my eye but it wasn't my tear. It was a tear from the eye of God.

On the Quad

Classes and exams continued to occupy a major portion of my time but this weekend there was going to be a concert on the Quad. I had learned that the last band was going to be a Christian band and this would be interesting. I took a mood enhancer earlier that afternoon to help me groove with the music. I listened to the first band and jammed away. The bands played and frankly I was a mess. When the Christian Band finally played, I heard the songs of Jesus and how he loved us and would change our old broken life into new life. And it hit me so hard, so devastating, right smack in the middle of my head, that I was being a hypocrite. I was telling people how Jesus came into my life but my actions were contrary to my new belief. How can that be, I thought? Right then, right now, I wanted to be off that high but I knew it would take hours for me to return to normal. I went home to my apartment, got under my blankets and I called Rod and Ray,

"Could you guys come over? I need to talk to you." They came over immediately and wondered what was going on and why I was in bed at 5 pm. With a sense of concern they asked,

"Are you sick, Dave? Should we get you to the hospital?" I began to recount my entire story of the day. I told them that I felt so repulsive. I was professing Jesus and I was stumbling right in the dirt.

"So what are you going to do Dave?" Rod said in a caring tone.

"I don't know exactly, but God is real to me. I just don't know where I am headed."

Sad and disconsolate of my failure, I vowed never to take any drugs like that again in my life. So many things had happened to me in this last month but God had touched me and I was beginning to learn that he wanted to use me not as a damaged vessel but a forgiven one.

I knew that for my light to shine, I had to clean up some things but I didn't know how. I knew I couldn't do it alone. I didn't even know that people had Bible studies. I wasn't going to go to some random church where I couldn't relate. So Rod and Ray were my pillars, although imperfect, yet they helped me see the Way.

> *Let your light shine before men, that they may see*
> *your good deeds and praise your Father in heaven.*
> *Matthew 5.16 NIV*

Rod, Ray, and Dave on a Road Trip

The Worst Letter Ever

There it was in the mail, a letter from the Selective Service. You are required to report in 30 days for you pre-induction physical in Chicago, Illinois. I was now down to about 125 lbs and truly a rail of a person. I had also been home to visit my longtime family doctor and he wrote me a note of whatever ailments might excuse my service. Although the letter was not very convincing, I would cling to any possible reason to be rejected. My physical was to be on a Thursday and I had a major chemistry exam on Friday morning. I asked my Professor if I could take my exam on Monday as I was taking a physical all day in Chicago. He promptly told me that I could drive myself down to Champaign Thursday night and take my exam first thing the next morning. I told him that I did not arrange the date of the physical and needed special consideration. He said that was not his problem. I said thank you and walked away.

I went home to Aurora late Wednesday and got ready for my physical. I prayed,

"Dear Lord, not my will but yours."

Early Thursday morning, I drove to the train depot in Geneva and got on the train to Chicago. I noticed all of the other young men on the train, no doubt headed to the same destination. I didn't know whether to just pray or begin to tell them about Jesus. I just sat and prayed.

The physical was an immediate joke to me. They might as well have shredded that letter from the doctor before I even presented it. I was now bordering 120 lbs and the realization poured through my consciousness, they did not care how much you weighed on either side of the spectrum. It was stupid that I put that much effort in to losing weight as though that might be a disqualifier. They checked my heart. I was breathing. Move to the next line.

"Everybody take off your clothes except your shorts and report in the next room." There must have been 50 men in our group and there were many other groups being processed in the surrounding rooms.

"Now drop your shorts and bend over." Are you serious I thought? Not that I had never been examined before and I understood that this might be part of the process. But, who gets a job with that job description? I must have passed my physical because there were no indications otherwise.

The train ride back to Geneva was long and lonely. This was

not the fate that I had prayed for. That "ask and you shall be given" didn't work out real well for me and the disappointment in myself and God was overwhelming. Why did I even think He cared? Could a God like this even exist? As the train car clacked down the tracks, the noise and vibration numbed me and there was not a word, nor a God who could fill that void I felt.

CHAPTER 20

Graduate School

I got rejection letters from Berkeley and Stanford. I made the Dean's list for Scholastic Excellence every semester at the UI. I thought I had a chance to make it into those two schools but I didn't. I think the blunder I unwittingly made during my senior research sealed that fate. I was extracting alkaloids from Ormosia Arborea and Ormosia Fastigiata beans and analyzing extracts by gas chromatography mass spectrometry. My professor had personally gone to the Amazon valleys to obtain these beans to look for anti-cancer and anti-tumor properties. In my zeal, I inadvertently used up every bean from this genus. I was scolded, demoralized by my research professor as he detailed my blatant error. I surely didn't get the ultimate glowing letter of recommendation from my research advisor that I had wanted. My last school UCLA had not written yet and although I had an assistantship from UCSB, I was still interested in UCLA. Finally, a letter in the mail came,

"You have been accepted into the graduate program in chemistry at the University of California, Los Angeles. We will provide you with a full Fellowship in addition to the standard Assistantship given to qualified students." Ok, I thought, drafted or go to school. Was that a choice? How do I plan?

I was getting a total full ride at UCLA and I was pumped. I wrote to UCSB and said I was no longer interested in their graduate program. I would be headed to California next summer to attend one of the finest schools in America with everything paid, my tuition, my housing, everything. My dream was going to come true. My first

93

challenge was complete. I graduated from the University of Illinois in June of 1971 with High Honors in Liberal Arts and Sciences and High Distinction in the Department of Chemistry. Sometimes I wonder if they had me confused with someone else. This young boy who never made the honor roll in high school, never participated in a single extracurricular event was now considered a scholar. I had worked hard for this day and I was ready for this dream to come true. I began planning for the summer and then dreaming about graduate school in the fall.

CHAPTER 21

Summer 1971

I packed all my bags for the last time. I was leaving my beloved University after 4 great years. The exams were tough, the friends were great, my activism born, and now a spiritual epiphany. I wasn't going to let the draft or the war spoil my summer. As I got in my car, I wondered how I would act when I saw my old friends wanting the old Dave to party like we used to.

I was going back to Aurora where I had made many of my worst decisions in my life. I drove my typical route from Champaign, west on Interstate 74, north on route 47 and then east on Alternate 30 into Aurora. On my way home I knew I had to stop at the home of Kathy Porter. I had come to know that Kathy was not only a wonderful girl of high principle, she was a Christian.

"Please be home, Kathy. Please be home," I whispered, as I knocked on her door.

"Kathy, it's for you," her sister said. I saw Kathy in the back room with a guy whom I thought was either her boyfriend or fiancée. I am not sure why I thought that but I didn't care. I just wanted to see Kathy.

"Dave!!!" Kathy shouted then smiled. Now Kathy had a smile that not only went from cheek to cheek but somehow lit up her eyes. I only had to look in Kathy's eyes and know every emotion going through that girl. Before she could utter another word, I said,

"Kathy I have found the Lord and I am scared." She took hold of both my hands and instinctively pulled them down so hard in excitement that our heads almost collided. We hugged and without saying another word, she knew. I told her of what had happened during the Spring. We sat down and talked.

"Kathy, I feel like I am so weak in my faith. One minute I am flush with excitement in knowing God and the next minute I wonder what fantasy world I am in now."

"How can I help you Dave?"

I said, "Pray, please pray for me Kathy." And we sat there praying. I knew she would pray for me the entire summer. I knew I could go to see her anytime I needed. But, I didn't and she knew I wouldn't.

I was only about 10 miles from my home and knew it was time to see my mom. But, I couldn't yet, I felt the urge, almost command, to go see Leann Spouts. I thought this was crazy. I haven't seen Leann for years and there really was nothing I was going to say. But I felt led to do this and as I drove into her empty driveway I said to myself, this is really dumb. I went up to the door and knocked. No answer. I knocked again and no answer. I went back to my car and as I was about to put the keys into the ignition, the door opened and I saw a young lady. It was Leann. I came up to the door and I could easily tell she had been crying.

"Leann, what's going on? Can I come in?"

"I'm sorry. Sure, come in." Leann said. After she gained her composure she continued, "Dave, I am so confused as to what is going on in my life. I was in my bathroom crying and I prayed that the Lord would send someone to help me."

I was stunned. I was absolutely amazed. It was never my intention to go to Leann's house. I had to change directions and I felt a little foolish going there. Yet, every time I felt like turning the wheel towards home, I sensed the gentle hand of God prompting me to go see Leann.

"Please tell me more, Leann. I want to hear."

"Dave, it's school, work, my future. I am so stressed out. I always felt close to God but now everything just seems empty."

Before I could say much more, her mom and brother came in and Leann introduced us. We had never met before and I am sure they both celebrated the day that Leann no longer had a romantic interest in me. There I stood, a long haired hippie with this reserved family. I sat down with Leann and shared everything that had happened to me. I told her all about the demonstrations and how I accepted Jesus into my life at a YWCA. Most of all I told her that the Lord wanted to work that same miracle in her life. She didn't quite see it that way and I understood. I then briefly spoke with her brother and mom on how God had touched me. And as I left, I could only think, "I planted the seed, Lord. Please send someone to water."

I was almost home now and I was excited. So much had happened on such a short trip of 3 hours. I made it home and began my summer of 1971.

Aurora

The very next day I knew what I was going to do. I went downtown where I always walked and socialized as a young high school student and began to ask everyone I met,

"Do you know if there are any Christians in this town?" I knew that in this town of over 80,000 that there were over 50 churches, maybe 100. We had Catholic churches, Presbyterian churches, Methodist churches, Lutheran churches, Pentecostal churches, and Baptist churches. I had seen them all. But as I walked the streets of Aurora, I could not remember a single person ask me or tell me about the person Jesus Christ. Not one. Nada.

As I asked this simple question, I wondered if people thought I was somewhat deranged. I could not imagine living a Christian life where I simply visited a fancy building on Sunday dressed in required fine attire. I knew that I would die like a flower in the sweltering heat. How could I find a group of young people who had experienced what I had? And so I continued in my old home town serious about questioning everyone I met,

"Do you know if there are any Christians in this town." After questioning so many strangers, I found someone I actually knew, a young fellow with long blonde hair that was as lost as I had been,

Jared Worby. We sat and talked inside the old S.S. Kresge store. At the food counter I shared my story with Jared and he shared with me about his interest in Eastern Religion. I didn't know Jared well and I never hung out with him but our circle of friends no doubt had touched many times. As I shared deeper into my story of the Christ who came into my life as a senior in college, he looked both interested and distant. I couldn't tell whether I was connecting with him. I think Jared had been in contact with other Christians because he said,

"I think I know what you are talking about. Go down to North Broadway beyond the old railroad roundhouse. By the river there is a garage called Gasoline Alley and ask for Jim." I thanked Jared and went down to Gasoline Alley. I asked for Jim and when he came back from the back of the shop I asked him,

"I hear you are a Christian, what do you do?" I am not sure what kind of question that was but Jim told me later that he thought I was crazy and maybe I would shoot him. I longed to hear that others had the same experience that I had and were active in their faith. I went to Jim's house that night and met his wife Ginger. Jim introduced me to Jerry Harvey and Will Ogden, two men who would have a profound influence in my life.

All of my old friends wanted me to get together with them and start up where we left off, partying, drinking, and smoking. At times I would succumb, knowing full well that they were pulling me away from the Lord. I shared with them that Jesus Christ had come into my life but they discounted that as total nonsense. Deep down in my heart I knew that I had to separate myself from them. I had hung out with these guys 6-10 years and the draw to continue that relationship was enormous. I was barely a Christian of three months and I had to make decisions that tore me apart. It took me almost half the summer and many mistakes to totally break those bonds.

My Family

It wasn't long after I got home that I went over to Lucy and Bob's home. Bob was Lucy's second husband. I liked Bob a lot as he always had a joke that put us in constant laughter. I knew I had a lot to say.

"I want you guys to sit down because I have some very important things to tell you."

"Why do we have to sit?" Lucy said somewhat defensively. That was not the reaction that I intended. I wanted to emphasize the profound importance of this conversation.

"No, you don't have to sit. I wanted to tell you that I found God in my life. He changed me and I can't explain what happened, just that it did happen." I recounted all the things that had happened to me in college and my chance encounter with a man from Campus Crusade. I shared with them the booklet titled the Four Spiritual Laws.

"I know it must be hard to absorb all of this, but please know that I am sharing this with both of you because I love you. I want you to understand that you can have new life, too." I left after that hoping that some of the things that I had said were meaningful to them. By the end of the month, I had spoken to my other sister Lonnie, my brother Phil, my mom, my cousin Peggy, and any family member who was willing to listen.

Living Waters Center

Jerry Harvey was a little older than me and had been studying at Trinity Divinity School. We had a small Bible study and out of that came the idea of starting a small center where young people could meet outside of the traditional church. We rented a small storefront on LaSalle Street about a block from the center of town. There was nothing special about this storefront as it probably was an old shoe repair shop. But we fixed it up and we began our Tuesday evening meetings at the Living Waters Center.

When we were not having meetings, we would often go out in the streets and share our faith. We had a small newspaper called the Hollywood Free Press that we would pass out. The personal evangelism seemed natural to me. Isn't this what Jesus commanded?

One evening as we went out I noticed an older man with us. He must have been 35. His hair was beginning to gray and I was curious how a man of that age would fit in with this new movement of young people. We were beginning to recognize ourselves as Jesus People, a younger generation sold out to God. Yet, as I was introduced to Will Ogden I knew that running deep through his veins was the same Gospel that I knew.

This particular evening we went to McCarty Park, between New York Street and Galena Boulevard. This area did not have great lighting and certainly people of questionable backgrounds gathered there. I came up to a dark haired young man and greeted him,

"Hi, my name's Dave and I want you to know that Jesus loves you."

"You don't know me," he said.

"I know that but could I give you one of these papers and maybe you could read it sometime."

He took the paper in one hand and looked directly at me. Then he took a big swig of his cola and proceeded to spit the entire contents onto the paper I had given him.

"Now that makes me feel good," he said in a mocking tone. He carefully watched for my reaction and I said nothing. I had about 20 of these newspapers in my hand. In complete silence, I began spreading each one out on the ground in a line extending about 5 feet. I said to him,

"If that made you feel good, then, go ahead and spit on the rest, and then maybe we can talk after that."

He didn't know what to do or say. I explained to him that Jesus loved him. He walked away without a word. Lord, touch that young man, I prayed. Will Ogden had watched this whole thing from a distance. He came by and prayed with me for that young man.

My Friends

I began to go downtown and share the Lord with the people I would meet. Sometimes I would go alone and sometimes as a group.

I don't know where I met Neil Wilson but he became a companion of mine as we shared about Jesus in the streets of Aurora. He had a friend, Ed, from Moody Bible Institute. They would come by together sometimes as late as 9:00 pm. We would pack our guitars and go play music out in the park or the shopping mall parking lots. Ed had an easel and he would do chalk talks explaining the gospel while Neil and I sang Christian songs. Neil was a straight laced kid with some association to Claim Street Baptist. I didn't know if he went there but it didn't matter. He was so on fire for the Lord that it surprised me. I think he also participated with the Navigators, a Christian college ministry. I really liked Neil and Ed possibly because they didn't fit my perception of what the Christian experience was. When we went out, I probably looked like John the Baptist and Neil looked like Luke, the physician. We both loved the Lord; we just had very different journeys.

I soon began to meet with many different Christian groups; from Wheaton, West Chicago, on-fire Catholics from St. Charles, and my best confidants: Will Ogden, Jerry Harvey, and Thurman Elkins. Of these three men, Will was my mentor, Jerry was my co-worker, and Thurman was my hero. Thurman was so humble of heart. He could speak into your soul without you feeling a bit defensive and then love you to death. I loved hearing him share the Gospel to young people. It was like rain on parched soil.

I would often go downtown Aurora on Saturday mornings just as I did in high school but now it was different. I was sharing the gospel with whomever I would meet. Some people would stop and talk while most would walk by pretending I didn't exist. One morning I met this elderly gentleman and I asked him,

"Do you know that Jesus loves you and that He has a plan for your life?"

"Please tell me more," he said.

I shared how Jesus, God in the form of man, gave His sinless life up that our sins might be forgiven. If we are willing to turn away from our old life, we can share a new life with our Creator. I spoke to him for several minutes telling him my story. Trying to give him an opportunity to speak I asked him,

"Do you go to church anywhere?"

He said, "Yes, I do, I go to Claim Street Baptist Church."

I said, "That is great. I have a good friend that goes out with me to share the Gospel and I think he goes to Claim Street Baptist. His name is Neil Wilson. I was at his wedding last weekend at your church. Do you know him or his family?"

"Yes, I do. His dad and I officiated his wedding."

I said, "I am so sorry. You should be preaching to me. If I have offended you in any way ..."

Pastor Adamson laughed, shook my hand, and said,

"I wasn't supposed to be the center of attraction anyways."

Several weeks later I saw Neil and I told him that I had met Pastor Adamson downtown and made a complete fool of myself. I was so embarrassed. Neil told me that Pastor Adamson had shared in his next service about this chance encounter with a young man on the streets of Aurora.

"I knew it was you." Neil told me. "Everything fit." He told me that Pastor Adamson asked his congregation how was it that this young man on the street was the only person that he had heard preach the Gospel in the streets of Aurora. I knew what Pastor Adamson was saying because no one had ever shared with me.

CHAPTER 22

The Trip Ahead

I had been a Christian less than 4 months and I had become a leader down at the Living Waters Center. At times I still had lingering doubts about what this whole life change really meant. For 21 years I had been this crazy young man and now for 4 months I was this reformed Christian. Summer was ending and I would soon be off to my next adventure, California.

I was ready to experience the next stage of my life. I imagined that graduate school would be tough, but I would make it through with the required scrapes and scabs. Somehow, I couldn't yet reconcile my new Christian life with my life dreams, but as a young man I just figured it would all work out. I mean there had to be Christians in California. As I planned my trip to California, the doubts of the whole Christian experience came roaring back that I wondered what was real and what wasn't. I felt my excitement for the Lord erode. I didn't know how I could blend it all with what lay ahead of me. It seemed that my whole life was in anticipation of going to California, seeing the babes on the beach, and getting my Ph.D. in chemistry.

I had a master plan. I would execute it and then see what happens. First go to Long Beach, California where I had a place to stay and then use that as a springboard to find an apartment close to UCLA. Mom was the last to see me before I left. She gave me those stares of love and worry that her baby boy, so confused in early life, was moving on and would not be home for a long time. She measured me like a cup of flour hoping that my new found faith was sufficiently sifted to withstand the coming battles. She did not yet understand the conversion that I went through but she knew I was different. Mom, concerned as always, quietly placed two bags of coins with at least $300 in the back seat of my car. We hugged and I looked around as to say good-bye to Aurora, bye to my home. I turned back to my mom and I couldn't help to see the tears swell in her eyes. As I struggled with my own, I said one last time, "I love you Mom."

I topped off my 1966 Pontiac Tempest with gas and I began my journey West. I headed toward Sugar Grove, then south on Hwy 47. On to Dwight, Illinois and there I settled in on Route 66. With my hands gripping the steering wheel and my eyes focused ahead, I couldn't erase the many questions that raced through my mind. I had worked with so many kids this summer and many had found a meaningful relationship with God. Yet, there were a fair number of them that walked away, back into their old life. They just quit their relationship with God and that was it. Could they get on with their old lives as if nothing had happened?

Was I doubting like Thomas? I don't think the Lord was mad or even disappointed in the Apostle Thomas. Thomas wanted his own experience. He wanted to see the Lord just like the other Apostles did. When the Lord came to Thomas, didn't He say, "Put your hands in my side and believe." And now I had begun to ask questions that I hadn't contemplated ever before. Were the last five months of my life a passing fancy that most people go through? Did I really want to be a Christian? Where was the Lord so that I could put my finger in the nail holes of His hands? I wanted to stay strong with the Lord but the prevailing winds were pulling me away. I wanted to be my own leader. It was my journey and I am the captain of my fate. I had messed up so many times … It was going to be a long trip.

I continued to motor westward on the most famous of all American highways spanning all the way from Chicago to Los Angeles, Route 66. I had mapped out my itinerary with a yellow highlighter pen on my road atlas, more than 2000 miles. I drove the first day from Aurora, through Saint Louis to the outskirts of

Tulsa, Oklahoma. It must have taken me about 11 hours. I picked up one hitchhiker along the way. We talked for awhile but I didn't feel really comfortable and dropped him off after 2-3 hours. I stopped at a truck stop that had a motel. I got a room for the night and went back to the truck stop diner.

"Hamburger, fries, and a soft drink," I said to the waitress.

I was usually not tongue tied. But, what was I supposed to say, 'I am tired, drove all day, kind of lonely, would you sit with me? I have all these questions that I don't have answers to.' That was never going to work, so I returned to my room and I prayed,

"Lord I am not sure what lays ahead of me, but please help me because I am a train wreck."

I got up early the next morning and headed out again. Oklahoma City, Amarillo, Albuquerque, and Gallup rolled by in the next 12 hours. The southwestern towns were separated by deserts and some of the most unique rock formations I had ever seen. Food, bathroom, and gas seemed to be the repetitive order of the day. For whatever reason, I didn't want to stop. It was late evening and I made it up to Flagstaff. The elevation was increasing and I would not even have realized that there were mountains around Flagstaff had not lightning lit the night time sky.

As I tired, I began to sing snippets from the Christian songs I had learned from the Bible. I was now past Needles, California and within 4 hours of Long Beach. My eyes were heavy but I wasn't going to give up now. I passed through San Bernardino at about 8 am. I was physically prying my eyes open to stay awake. I drove 23 hours that day. I swore on my mother's grave that I would never drive that road, that distance again by myself. I was exhausted and I was going to sleep all day and all night but I was happy. I arrived.

CHAPTER 23

It Pours in Southern California

Here I was in Long Beach, California in a bug infested apartment about two miles from the beach. I was going to stay for about one month. One night as I was sleeping, I felt a cockroach crawl across my face toward my mouth. I grabbed that cockroach and threw it as hard as I could against the wall and stomped on it as hard as I could. I was disgusted. My faith was similarly crashing. It seemed so lonely in sunny Southern California. I went out for a drive and saw that bumper sticker on my car that said, "Jesus is the Answer." I had no answers and I wanted to rip off that sticker and shred it into little pieces.

I started going to the beaches in Long Beach, Venice and Santa Monica. I would just walk and walk. When the waves were large, I would body surf and pretend I was part of the Southern California crowd. On the way to the beach in Long Beach, I passed Our Savior's Lutheran Church. I saw young people playing volleyball and just having a good time. I didn't know if these were college kids or high school kids. I decided to stop. When they asked me to join them, it felt like salve on a festering wound. I soon realized they were high school kids. I began to spend time with the youth pastor who was about my age and we talked a lot about our Christian experiences. I needed someone, a person to talk with me.

Early one evening, I was sharing with the youth group a portion of my story and how I had come to California. There were many questions, even relating to doctrine. I hadn't noticed that one of the senior pastors was listening carefully. It was his flock and I had no intention but to love Jesus and love them. He wanted to know what my training was and I told him, I only read the bible and only became a Christian this very year. I think he liked me but he needed me to become more involved in the specifics of Lutheran theology if I were to continue to work with the youth group. I perfectly understood. I knew before long I would soon be moving on to school. So not too long afterwards I told the youth group that I would soon be moving to attend UCLA graduate school. We prayed together and I got some of the most sincere hugs that I can remember.

I regularly visited Westwood where UCLA was located and looked for housing. I would look at the information boards and local papers for apartments. I thought it would be better if I could sublet a room in a house. After several days I hadn't found anything and I was getting seriously tired of looking. I wanted to live close to campus if possible. I was surprised by the concrete jungle and the largely urban setting of what was the UCLA campus. It was right next to Beverly Hills.

Venice Beach

I was quickly approaching the point where I no longer knew what I was searching for. My life was conflicted as I fought between my dreams and my reality. I had left Illinois with no attachments. There were no beautiful women begging me to come home. I had emotionally separated myself from my family and felt no reason to return. I didn't really know where I belonged. So here I was in California, reeling like a ship with no destination.

I finally found a place, a one room efficiency in Venice, California about a block from the beach. The room was about 12x20 feet, enough for a twin bed, a small table, a bathroom, an efficiency kitchen, a chair, and a television. I truly struggled with this location because I knew there were a lot of drugs and crazies around, especially at night. But, it was less than 30 minutes from UCLA. I had been in California about three weeks now and had about two weeks before I registered for classes at UCLA. For the next few days,

I would walk the beach in the morning, come home, take a shower, veg a little, and then walk the Venice Boardwalk at night.

Yes, I was here in sunny Southern California, a young Christian man trying to find his way. I wasn't making any friends yet and I was trying to desperately hold onto my faith. The refrain from the song Eleanor Rigby by the Beatles riddled me, "All the lonely people, where do they all come from?"

Where did I come from and where do I belong? My struggles were just now beginning. After swimming on a sunny afternoon, I began my trek through the soft sand of Venice Beach. There often were sunbathers on the beach but not that many this day. As I began walking towards my one room efficiency, it was not hard to notice this young lady sunbathing topless on the beach. She was in no way, shape, or form embarrassed about her body but seemed rather pleased with her endowment. My only question was, how close do I walk by her? Do I stop and talk to her? I came close enough that I could describe her in quite detail, close enough to amplify my mental turmoil. I did not stop to talk. But, I did look. It was a long hard look.

The Bible says to flee youthful lusts and yet I couldn't. I didn't have the strength and I wasn't sure if I wanted to. I recalled the story of Joseph in the Land of Egypt and how he escaped Potiphar's wife.

> *One day Joseph went into the house to attend to his duties, and none of the household servants was inside. She caught him by his cloak and said, 'Come to bed with me!' But he left his cloak in her hand and ran out of the house. Genesis 39:11-12 NIV*

But I wasn't Joseph. I didn't want to be Joseph! I just hurt inside. The question that nagged me, that dogged me, that followed me, nipping my feet each day as I came to the beach, "Why did you come to California? Isn't this what you wanted?" The answer was straightforward. First, I came to California to experience the beach life and enjoy women just like the ones that travelled this beach. Second, I was coming to California to get my doctorate. I had sacrificed months and years doing laborious work to be here. Right here. Now I find God at the YWCA in Champaign, Illinois, and everything is different. I don't want everything to be different. And all I can say is it's my dream, my life, my future. And I am not sure I wanted anybody telling me what to do. But then, why did I ask God to help me? Did His friendly advice come with a choice?

On the Boardwalk

The next evening I went to the Venice Boardwalk. The Venice Boardwalk is laced with colorful buildings, some in disrepair. There was an older amusement park that appeared to be mostly abandoned. It had paid deeply from the ravages of the salt and winds of an ocean. The pedestrian walkway was over two miles long and I was living on the edge of the worst part of town. During the days, kids on roller skates would freely travel the boardwalk. Joining them were the street merchants, mystics, and tourists. At night, marijuana and drugs became more evident. One building housed a Christian Outreach Center and I wanted to visit. I could only hope for some kind of bond.

The center was pretty barren. It had a few older chairs and a couple of posters on the walls. It was almost depressing, but maybe the nightly visitors liked it.

"We are trying to reach those who are lost in chemical addictions. We get some pretty strung out people in here. Are you from around here?"

"I am living off the boardwalk in an apartment just south of here but originally I am from Illinois," I said.

"You got roommates."

'No, I'm by myself."

"Hmmm, not good," he said.

Hmmm, not good is all he said. I guess I knew that God was

trying to show me something but I was I too entrenched in my dreams to hear Him out.

"Hey, Man," a stranger said. "I am from Neptune." The man was clearly high on drugs and his parched skin was indicative of sleeping outdoors, probably right on the boardwalk.

"How did you get here," I asked trying to engage in some sort of conversation.

"Waves, baby, waves."

"You mean by the Ocean," I interrupted.

"Intergalactic waves, electromagnetic field gradients. Space, baby, space. I am on a trip and they sent me here. CIA is after me."

I left the center knowing that I was ill prepared to help. I went to my apartment just wondering how I got here. Was God real? It sure didn't feel like it. I felt so close to God just a month ago at the Living Waters Center in Aurora, but here I am drying up like a flower in the desert, just like the one I drove through. Wasn't God supposed to prepare a way? Here I am in the desert wilderness, living my dream in sunny Southern California, and it is pouring rain on me.

San Bernardino Mountains

This afternoon I saw a group of young people passing out Christian flyers. Many of the girls were dressed in hippie tie-dye dresses and the guys in simple t-shirts and bell bottom jeans. I felt my countenance lift a little because I had been very involved with similar groups in Illinois. Somehow, this seemed a little different.

A man about my age came up to me and said,

"What's your name?"

"Dave, and yours?"

"Michael"

"Michael, could you tell me a little bit about your group." I asked.

"We are an evangelistic group sharing the Gospel of Jesus Christ. We share each day and those that would be inclined, we invite to our ministry center for dinner."

Dinner, I thought. I have not had a decent dinner in almost 4 weeks. Fast food and the garbage I make are about all I eat.

I began asking a lot of questions. "How does it work? Where is the center?

He said, "Our team will be picked up at 4:30 at the corner. We are in San Bernardino. Why don't you join us?"

"And how do I get back?"

"We'll give you a ride."

I thought about it and I said to myself, I need some good Christian fellowship. I need to meet some people here in California. I came back at 4:30 and saw the team. They were quiet. They looked tired and disheveled. I was alert and ready to talk. I saw Michael and had him assure me again that I would get a ride back. Off we went. The team now appeared to be like zombies from shear exhaustion. I couldn't figure out the disconnect. Weren't Christians supposed to be happy and have the out flowing of the living God? We passed cities I didn't recognize and almost 90 minutes later we were deep in the San Bernardino Mountains.

The bus pulled into the compound alongside a number of other buses. The road was dusty, begging for rain and I wondered what adventure lay before me. In the distance there were long buildings that appeared to be the sleeping barracks for the team. There was another large building which doubled as the kitchen-dining area and the meeting area. I was invited in and I saw a good number of people, at least 200. I couldn't tell the difference between the guests and residents. I sat down at a table and waited for the prayer. After I got my food cafeteria style, I took my chair again. I was getting apprehensive as to where I actually was and what was I doing here.

As I sat down to eat, I felt like I was in a speed dating line waiting for the next person to sit by me and interrogate me. It was the same questions, "Where am I from?" "Do you really know the Lord?" As the evening progressed I found out from one of the leaders that the "Lord" had revealed to them that He was going to return right here in the San Bernardino Mountains and claim His Bride for the new Millennium. I knew better than that. There was no reason to argue. It was their house and their rules.

The service was about to begin and I was shown to a seat.

"Now when our Leader gives an altar call, you need to go down and kneel at the front."

After telling them countless times that I had accepted the Lord and I didn't need to go forward, I began to tire. I knew they were involved with a form of brainwashing and emotional coercion. I needed a ride home so I didn't want to agitate anyone. I had no clue whatsoever where I was. I went forward and they were all pleased. I wondered if they got a commission for their success.

Then the kicker came, "This is God's new home for you and if you leave here, you will surely lose your salvation." The peer pressure was immense but I knew better. I wasn't going to respond, I just stated I needed to go home and pray. With reluctance they put me on the bus and we passed the dusty roads of the compound, back down the mountains, back to Venice, California.

CHAPTER 24

Through It All

As I sat on my bed in my little Venice apartment, my thoughts gradually began to crystallize. All the reasons that I came to California were tarnished by my selfishness. Those dreams about meeting beautiful women and going to the finest schools were indeed strong. They controlled me. They were the passion within me that brought me here, that kept me in school, that kept me from totally succumbing to the drug scene. It was a passion of personally reaching a pinnacle of accomplishment and now one that I could no longer reconcile with my new Christian beliefs.

From my days in high school, throughout my time at the University of Illinois, a total of 7 years I had dreamed of the day I would be here in California. Now, I had a full fellowship and assistantship at one of the most prestigious schools in America, UCLA. It was going to be a whole new way of life, something exceptional. But, something happened to me. I had found the Lord. And these questions that ran through my mind tormented me. How do I surrender my dreams, each and every one? How do I lay them all down?

I got down on my knees and I began to pray. I had to make a decision bigger than I ever had before. And the instantaneous moment I knew I was quitting all and coming home to Illinois, my heart leaped just like the day I was saved.

David Valdez

But whatever was to my profit I now consider loss for the sake of Christ. What is more, I consider everything a loss compared to the surpassing greatness of knowing Christ Jesus my Lord, for whose sake I have lost all things. I consider them rubbish, that I may gain Christ and be found in Him. Phillipians 3:7-9 NIV

CHAPTER 25

Going Home

I went into the chemistry department office at UCLA and told them I would not be entering school. They wanted me to speak with the head of the department but I declined knowing that he would only try to convince me to stay. I could not do that. I cleaned out my apartment and turned in my keys. That very day I began to retrace my steps as I got into my car bound for Aurora, Illinois.

It was a little over a month ago that I had vowed never again to drive that distance alone. Here I was driving back, but with a slight change of direction. There were people I needed to see. I would first go to Boulder, Colorado and then Iowa City. Through the deserts of California, Arizona, and New Mexico I traveled, but this time with a song in my heart. It was the end of September and I had barely been a Christian 6 months. I felt old and punished from all the turmoil but now I was refreshed. I spent the first night in a rest stop in New Mexico. I just locked the door and fell asleep until the morning sun woke me. I began going north. I had just entered Colorado when I heard on the radio that the Selective Service Board would only take up to number 125 in the draft.

"Hallelujah, Praise the Lord," I shouted out loud in the car and out the windows. Though no one was there to hear my screams of joy, I was sure that I could hear the echoes tumbling down the mountain passes. My number was 129. I would not be drafted. I would never be drafted. And as I thought about this, I wondered that if I had heard this one week ago, would I have stayed in California? And what if I heard it yesterday, would all of my plans have changed?

But, no, I heard it today and I was convinced that God had me on a journey, a fantastic journey of life.

I stopped in at the University of Colorado to see Terri, a good friend, who had lived in St. Charles, Illinois. I told her about my experience in California and how I felt God was leading me home. I left Colorado the next morning to go to the University of Iowa to see Leann one last time. I recalled how the Lord led me to her home and how I had shared with her my new faith. I arrived at her sorority and they said she was down at one of the local bars. I found the bar, it was crowded. How different it felt. I was no longer comfortable with the heavy drinking and loud music which had been a core destination within my soul. I looked down past the bar stools. I saw Leann sitting in a booth with a couple of guys. She looked at me squinting her eyes not sure what she was actually seeing,

"Dave?"

"Yeah Leann, it's me. I guess you are kind of surprised."

"Well, I wasn't expecting to see you here, but I am glad. What are you doing here?"

I don't know if Leann thought I wanted to rekindle a relationship or I had just gone crazy. But I had to share the Lord with her one more time.

"Leann, I know you think I am nuts. I was this crazy freaked out kid who has done so many things wrong. Remember when I came to your house at the beginning of summer? I told you that when Jesus came into my life, I changed. I wanted to tell you again because you have been special in my life."

"I know Dave, and you have been special too. I was so glad you came to see me but I have grown and I am enjoying my life here at Iowa."

"I can see that Leann. I don't mean to sound repetitive. I just wanted to tell you that one astonishing day in the midst of my confusion, I asked Jesus in my heart and if you ask him, he will come into your heart, too."

We could have talked longer but I knew by now that when a person is not ready to hear Jesus, talking was just a noisy static.

"Dave, it's almost 11 pm. Why don't I find you a place to stay here in Iowa City, one of the frats maybe?"

"I can't Leann. Home is less than 4 hours away and I can make it before the dawn."

I drove home that night. I was at peace. I could only imagine what it would be like the next few days. I arrived in the wee hours of the night. I had told my mom I was coming home so I wouldn't alarm her. I quietly came in and fell asleep on the living room floor. At dawn, Maria, my young cousin whom I really loved, sat down beside me while I was sleeping. I think she just stared until I blinked my eyes. She said,

"Dave, Dave, I am so glad to see you." I awoke and I gently kissed her on the forehead. I then got up and saw my mom. She scolded me again on how I should have stayed in school. But she wasn't mad; she was just being my mom. I loved being home. It's where I belong.

CHAPTER 26

The Surprise Letter

It wasn't until Saturday Afternoon that I was refreshed from the long drive. I knew I had to get back to the Living Waters Center on LaSalle Street. I arrived about 7 pm and as I walked down the steps into the Center, I heard a chorus of,

"Dave, you're back. You're back."

I quickly embraced my friends whom I had deeply missed. Out of the corner of my eye I noticed a new face. There was this young brown haired girl with men's orange work boots and pigtails. She was about my age and I thought to myself how beautiful she was. But, what enthralled me the most were those work boots and pigtails. I went up to her and said,

"Hi, my name is Dave."

She said, "My name is Judy." I later learned that she was a second year teacher at Simmons Junior High School in Aurora and she worked with children with disabilities. We sang choruses of songs that night and the one I loved the most was,

I have decided to follow Jesus.
I have decided to follow Jesus.
Though none go with me,
Still I will follow.
No turning back, No turning back.

"Dave, we are having a party, a small get together at my house tomorrow night. We'd love for you to come," Dorothy said. Dorothy was one of the regulars at the Living Waters Center.

"Oh Yeah, I wouldn't miss it." I will come, but I thought to myself, I really hope Judy is there.

I looked at Judy and said, "Are you going to come, we would really like to see you." I didn't want to say I would really like to see you. That might be too forward, but I did want to see her again.

"I will try to be there," she said.

I couldn't wait for Sunday night to come. I got over to Dorothy's and Judy was there. Yes, she was! I could barely contain myself. As I ate finger foods and talked with everyone, I kept gravitating toward this new girl, Judy Moschel. As I made my way through the room, each step was calculated to get a little closer until I arrived right next to her and I kind of nonchalantly said,

"Oh, Hi Judy. I am glad you came." Every moment I was with her was almost transcendent to this mortal. At this same time I didn't know what she was thinking. How could I? This was only the second time I had even seen her. I kind of thought she was attracted to me. As the evening progressed, I noticed that Judy looked a little worried. She confided in me,

"Dave, I am a new Christian and earlier tonight this guy came up to me and told me that God had told him I was going to marry him. What I am I supposed to do?"

I asked her if this was John who said this. She said, "Yes."

"Well, you are not the first one this has happened to. God always lets you participate in your journey. So, I would not concern myself at all. God has a plan for your life and it isn't being told to you through a stranger."

We talked and laughed throughout the evening at this party. I hardly noticed anyone else there. I went home. I was living at my sister Lonnie's home on Root Street at this time. The next morning when I woke up there was note on my windshield. It must have been left the evening before.

Smile, God Loves You,
The Lord does have us scheduled on Monday.
How 'bout coming to supper on Tuesday?? (unless the Lord has other
plans ...) PTL!!
In Christ,
Judy

How did she know where I lived and how did she know it was my car? I must have said something. I was so excited. I couldn't help but think about the two special letters I had received in my life. First, the sweet letter I got from Amy in the second grade learning about the postal system, and then the card from Kathy Porter. How I cherished that letter. I put it in my guitar case and there it was for years. Now I have this third letter, and I can barely contain myself.

Of course I will come to dinner. It isn't often that you get invited to dinner after meeting someone just two days earlier, especially someone so attractive who wears work boots and pigtails. I loved it! I put that card in my wallet and there it lay for years. It was mine forever.

I learned that Judy had been living with the Lenka twins since their mom had been sick and was in the hospital. That night Judy made a macaroni cheese hot dish. To this day I never remember macaroni and cheese tasting so good. I thought to myself that this must be some recipe handed down from multiple generations. But, there it was on the kitchen counter, a box of mac-n-cheese. I think there was something else going on in my mind.

Every night that week, I went over to see Judy at the Lenka's house and we all ate together. Every night I would tell the girls Bible stories before they went to bed. Then Judy and I would talk until the wee hours of the evening. She told me about her job at Simmons Junior High School and her summer work at Big Bay, Michigan. There was a camp for disabled children right on the shores of Lake Superior just north of Marquette, Michigan. When she talked about the children there, a light radiated brightly from her face. She told me that she never cared if she got paid and didn't even know how much she was paid. I was surprised at first, but her eyes expressed what true passion was. And each evening when she knew how much sleep she would not get, she would say good night and I would go home.

"Dave, a bunch of us are going up to Big Bay, Michigan over Columbus Day weekend. We will be picking up some friends along the way and there is room for you in the car. Would you like to come?"

I didn't even have to think about it. Lake Superior ... Big Bay, Michigan ... Judy Moschel!!!

"I would love to go. What do I need to bring?"

CHAPTER 27

Big Bay Michigan

The weekend came and we got in Judy's lime green Oldsmobile F-85. We must have talked the whole way to Madison, Wisconsin where we picked up her friend Sharon. I began to drive her car as we headed to Marquette in the Upper Peninsula of Michigan. It was at that point when I put my hand in her hand that I knew something special was happening. I mean most guys have held girl's hands, but there is something magical when that moment is transcendent. Tonight it was. I knew this girl 6 days and I was falling in love.

We made it up to Marquette and picked up Micha, another friend of Judy's. We were now off to Big Bay, Michigan. Big Bay is located northeast of Lake Independence and south of Lake Superior. People from the Upper Peninsula of Michigan make a special effort to let you know that they are not from the mainland of Michigan. They are Yoopers.

We made our way through the dirt roads to our weekend cabin arriving after midnight. Right on the shores of Lake Superior was her friend's cabin, the Tilton Hilton. It was a rustic cabin nestled in the backwoods of Lake Superior. The view of Lake Superior from the cabin was spectacular especially in the moonlit sky. There was a main room where you cooked and hung out. Then there was one bedroom and a loft. There was an outhouse about 30 feet from the cabin. I wasn't prepared to use it in the middle of the night but there were no other options. The whole group of us got our sleeping bags and slept wherever we could. A number of us slept up in the loft. Judy was close enough to me that I could hold her hand as we went to sleep.

I was not sure what was going through Judy's mind at the time. I loved her flannel shirts, her love of the outdoors and her long brown hair. I loved that she had a heart for children and adults with disabilities. We all woke up early and had breakfast that Saturday morning. A large group of Judy's camp friends hiked with us to a lookout called Breakfast Roll in the Huron Mountain Club. The fall leaves had begun to show their splendor of orange, yellows, and reds. The views were spectacular!

That evening we met with more of her friends that she had worked with at Baycliff Health Camp. They asked her what she had been doing and how she had met me. Judy looked at me and then she began to share her story of how she found Christ. I remembered how I had seen an article in the Aurora Beacon News about three teachers who had found new faith and were now working at Simmons Junior High School. The article was posted at the St. Gregory Book Shop and at the time I pondered whether I would ever meet them. Judy continued to share with her friends about her love of God and how He was moving in her life. After a great evening in Big Bay we went back to the Tilton Hilton. It was Sunday night.

Everyone had gone back into the cabin except Judy and me. We sat outside on the picnic table and talked for a long time and there I kissed her. Hand in hand we walked slowly down to the Lake. We sat down on one of the large rocks and listened to the water softly lap upon the shore. I was with this young lady that I had only known 8 days and suddenly I stopped everything I was doing, everything I was thinking, and I looked straight into her eyes and said,

"Judy Moschel, will you marry me?"

I had gone to California in search of the perfect woman. She wasn't there, she was right here with me. And though I wasn't sure why or how I could ask her to marry me after only 8 days, I did. There it was out in space, a heartfelt question of astronomical proportions. It wasn't do you love me, nor was it could we date exclusively. Nope, it wasn't would you like to meet my parents. It was 'will you marry me.' And I didn't say; Oh, by the way I don't have a ring. I don't have a job. I don't have an apartment. I'm just living at my sister's house. And my mom owns a pool hall, Hustler's Pool Hall on Claim Street. Nope, I just said from the deepest part of my heart to the girl of my dreams,

"Judy Moschel, will you marry me?"

And though a lot of time hadn't passed it felt like eternity. I watched as she formed her words,

"Yes, I will marry you Dave!"

I am not sure who surprised who more, me asking or Judy saying yes. But there it was, a night I would never forget. And there we were somehow totally smitten after 8 days, totally given to each other and convinced that we would soon be married.

"Dave, do you remember the cross that you gave me a couple days ago?"

"Yeah, I bought one for myself too." I had purchased two identical crosses from St. Gregory bookshop hoping that she would wear one and I would wear the other.

"Do you know what those two intersecting rings on the cross mean?" Judy asked.

"Not really?"

"They're a symbol of marriage, of life, and the two rings are forever attached to each other. Did you know that when you gave it to me?"

"Mmm, no, but I should have. I know it is how I feel. I love you and I want to be married to you for the rest of our lives."

Judy kissed me softly. I don't know how things like this happen. You can't plan it. You can't will it. You just watch the unfolding of the most beautiful events in life. Even though we were both scared, we both were so sure that we were meant to be. We drove back to Aurora, Illinois on Monday knowing that we had a lot of talking and planning to do.

Note, Crosses, and Rings

CHAPTER 28

Meeting Judy's Parents

It wasn't long after we decided to get married that Judy said we needed to go meet her parents. I thought it was a good idea, we needed to do it. Now Judy came from a conservative Midwestern background. Her father, Don, had served in World War II and won the Silver Medal for bravery in combat in the Pacific theater. He also was awarded the Purple Heart. Don was a pipefitter and owned some small businesses. He took no gruff from anyone, he had earned his right to speak on any issue. Judy's mom was reserved and a hard worker as well. It seemed that most parents that had gone through the Great Depression knew that only by their own hard work could they succeed. Two jobs per person was not the exception, in many families it was the norm.

"Let me change into something a little more respectable," I said. I had on a pair of bell bottom jeans with a green work t-shirt with the small pocket in the front. In the back of the t-shirt was a gaping hole you could put your head through. Over that mess, I was wearing a brown suede leather jacket that was two sizes too big for me.

"Don't be so nervous. They just want to meet you." They just want to meet me I think. My thoughts began to batter my brain. My hair is a long Afro. I am dressed like an impoverished street musician and I shouldn't be nervous. "Take a deep breath," I say to myself. She knows her parents better than me.

We arrived at Judy's parents' home and there were cars in the driveway, cars in the street, cars down the street, and all I was thinking about is, 'I have a t-shirt on with a hole in the back as big as my head.' We walked in the door and just as I had suspected when we parked the car, Judy's mom and dad were having a family party. Judy's mom was the first to greet us,

"Come in, come in."

"Hi Mom, I want you to meet Dave. Dave, this is my mom"

"Hello, Mrs. Moschel, pleased to meet you."

"Bern or Bernice is fine. Could I take your coat as it is a little warm in here."

"Ummm, no, I prefer to have it on if that's ok?"

"Oh please let me take it," she said as she grabbed my arm to take off my coat. Now I am thinking, 'which of a thousand deaths would be better than to totally embarrass myself on the first visit to the Moschel family.' I wasn't sure if Judy was shaking because she knew my dilemma or she was trying not to laugh.

"I am ok now but if I get too warm, I will surely take it off."

I made it through the first set of questions. Where are you from? Where did you grow up? Where did you go to school? Where are you working? How did you meet? I exhale. I think the hardest part was that we met at the Jesus Center. Judy's mom and her sisters had a strong Catholic background and were unsure of this new young man. I still think they liked me! Judy's family was a very tight knit group. Some of her uncles voiced strong opinions but they were great guys. One thing for sure, they adored their niece and certainly wanted to grill the fellow she dragged home. Judy had nine aunts and many were there. They were all very nice to me, especially Aunt Jo, Aunt Lori and Aunt Eleanor. Judy had so many aunts and uncles I couldn't keep track of them all. I knew my Aunt Mary and that was it.

We hadn't yet told her parents about our engagement and tonight was not a good night. But it would be soon, real soon.

CHAPTER 29

Hallelujah Dave

Being engaged, I had never done that before and I really didn't know what the expectations were. I knew I was madly in love with Judy Moschel and believed that she was in love with me. But as usual I was pretty ignorant on important issues other than I was pretty sure I needed a job. You sort of come from living with your parents, going to school, and then of all the mean tricks in life, you gotta get a job, especially if you're getting married. And that I was!

I began scanning the papers and came up empty. Judy was teaching at Simmons Jr. High School on Sheffer Road at the time and we both found it funny and interesting that I had lived so close to that school as a boy. Finally, a job as security personnel at East Aurora High School was posted in the paper. Not quite the field of chemistry, but it was just for the school year. It was mid October, 1971, and I was going to apply. One of the interviewers was John Hinck, the Superintendent of East Side School District 131.

"David Valdez," Mr. Hinck said.

"Yes Sir, Mr. Hinck," I replied.

Without missing a beat as though it a happened yesterday, Mr. Hinck said,

"David Valdez, Hermes Elementary School, the fourth grade."

Although I never had Mr. Hinck for a class, he ran the intramural program after school and on Saturday morning. We would play basketball, dodge ball, and gymnastics. How he remembered me, I don't know. Maybe it was when he plastered me playing dodge ball. I was trying to sneak up on him and surprise him but guess who got surprised and got nailed a good one? I think he felt bad about that but somehow it kindled a wonderful memory that neither of us forgot. But it still was quite surprising for him to remember me 12 years later. I got the job and I was to begin immediately.

I didn't really understand what the job entailed, but as young person "engaged to be married" I was glad I to get a job, any job. I mean you need some sort of respectability, especially to your new in-laws. Hey, what was I going to say?

"I want to marry your daughter, I don't have a job and I live at my sister's house. Could you lend me some money for a ring? Yeah, and your daughter is going to support me." Oh my, that's a great start!

The first day of work, I parked my car in the staff parking lot, and there I met Clarence and Bill. They were two older men that had the same job. They probably confused me for a student. I was 21 years old and always looked young for my age. I wasn't but a few years older than many of the students and some of them undoubtedly could grow a beard better than I. There wasn't much formal training from Clarence or the Dean of Students.

Just keep the kids in order.
Bring the unruly to the Dean's office.
Prevent contraband, mostly drugs and marijuana, from permeating the building.

I can do that, I thought. As I stood in the midst of these students, I couldn't help but think that only a few years before I had walked the halls at West Aurora High School without direction or purpose. The salary, $550 per month, for the new job was meager but it gave me a morsel of respectability. But more so, it placed me smack dab in the middle of 1,500 students who needed me not as a hallway security monitor, but as a friend and a voice of someone who was so lost and now had been found. It was so profound to me, God had placed me in their midst to be a friend and a witness of Him. But, there were so many students. And I was reminded that when Jesus saw the crowds, he had compassion on them.

> *Jesus went through all the towns and villages, teaching in their synagogues, preaching the good news of the kingdom and healing every disease and sickness. When he saw the crowds, he had compassion on them, because they were harassed and helpless, like sheep without a shepherd. Then he said to his disciples, "The harvest is great, but the workers are few. Ask the Lord of the Harvest, therefore to send out workers into his harvest field." Matthew 9:35-38 NIV*

There I was in the midst of the harvest. I began to speak and share with whomever would listen in the halls of East Aurora High School. Most were pleasant and willing to engage in most any conversation. I shared how I was a confused young man walking the streets of Aurora and one day as a senior in college the most amazing thing happened. God came into my life and changed me forever. Some were skeptical but some actually knew the old me or someone in their family knew me.

I met Stacey Neville, a short redheaded young lady as I walked the halls. Short only because I was 6'2" tall and anyone under 5'4" was short. Stacey was blind from birth which was easy to tell as she navigated the halls with her white cane. Her slow gait and cumbersome books of Braille were characteristic of the depth of her disability.

"Would you like to take my arm? I would be honored to walk with you to class." Now today that would probably be frowned upon, a student taking the arm of an employee in the middle of school. But in 1971 no one seemed to notice or really care.

"Who are you?" Stacey said in a careful soft tone. Stacey would often need help but certainly had been warned of strangers.

"My name is David Valdez and I am an employee of the school. It is my job to make the hallways safe and accessible to all students."

Daily she took my arm and I walked her to third period class. We spoke about her classes, her hopes and ambitions. My life with Jesus and how He changed me always entered the conversation. Sometimes I would just casually bring something up about the Living Waters Center or she would initiate questions about Jesus. One day as I was talking to her I mentioned that I was painting a room in the apartment we had just rented from our new landlady, Mrs. Putt. Judy and I were not married yet but we were decorating our future apartment on West Park Avenue.

"I can help you paint, Mr. Valdez. I really can. I know how to paint."

I thought very carefully about this and I said, "If it is ok with your parents, I will talk it over with Judy." And so with everyone's permission Stacey came over to paint. We helped guide her hands and her sense of accomplishment highlighted my weekend. Judy had a special talent with individuals with special needs and knew every aspect of helping that I sorely lacked. More and more, not only Stacey but others began to know that my job at East Aurora High School was more than a job. It was a ministry, a mission of love and understanding given to me. Surely it was not known to the administrators of the school district. Little did they know of God's plans for me. So every day, I walked the parking lots and halls of East Aurora High School speaking with boldness waiting to see God's hand move in this school.

"Hallelujah Dave," came a whisper behind me. I couldn't tell who it came from as the hallways were crowded with students bustling between classes. I didn't think much about it because I was sure that of the many names students had for me, there were many far worse than this. The next day came another voice just a little louder,

"Hallelujah Dave." I quickly turned but to no avail. Was that the name that the students had finally settled on giving me? I began to realize that many of them thought that this might be a way to push one of my buttons. Anything they could do to make fun of me was fair game and they were having a great time calling me "Hallelujah Dave." I knew they were laughing, but I was too. It was warmth to my soul.

The next day taped on the foyer wall was a picture. I had pulled down all types of pictures from the walls this year. Some were quite offensive, but this was different. On the wall was an effervescent hippie stick-figure standing on one foot, his hands in the air, and a Bible in one hand with the caption, "Hallelujah Dave." I laughed to myself as I pulled the picture off the wall and stuffed it in my pocket. The whispers continued as an orchestrated gesture by a small segment of the student body.

"Hallelujah Dave," I would hear but I never turned to see who it was anymore. I never felt diminished or that I was being mocked. Quite the contrary I thought to myself. What better name could I ever be given? That which was meant for mischief, was actually a soothing breeze into my soul. I could only imagine going to the Pearly Gates of Heaven and seeing St. Peter. He would ask,

"Who are you?" As he was checking names that were written in the Book of Life.

And I would holler, "It's Hallelujah Dave!" Not being sure in this solemn moment if I should be raising my voice or not.

And Peter would say, "John, James, Mark. Come over here. Hurry! It's Hallelujah Dave! Bring the Picture."

"A couple of kids came up a few days ago, knocked on the gate. They said they knew you and heard the message of our Lord. They brought this picture and said Hallelujah Dave will soon be here."

"Well, here I am and that's me!" I shouted, excited to see all the heroes of my faith.

Hallelujah Dave at the Pearly Gates

To many of the kids, I was just a crazy hall monitor who had somehow invaded their world. But to me this was the where I was supposed to be, right in their midst. So many of them had experienced many of the things that I had: divorced parents, alcohol and drug use. And every night I would go to Judy's apartment to tell her all the things that happened to me that day. Judy would love to hear my stories and she would tell me hers. But, the inevitable would have to happen. One of the counselors called me into his office.

"Do you know Johnny Carpenter?"

"Yes, I do," knowing full well where this conversation was going. I had met John in the halls and we had spoken many times about the Lord. His family was not religious and he wanted to know more about Jesus.

With a troubled voice the counselor told me, "His mother called me and frankly she is not very happy. She said that you were influencing him with talk about Jesus. Are you?"

My heart dropped. I didn't want to lose this job, but my heart was so sold out to these kids. I said,

"Yes, we talk about a lot of things in the hallway. Among them is our personal faith. I did not coerce him or anyone to listen. We just talk."

"I am not in favor of these conversations," admonished the counselor in a tone that was not open for discussion. "They need to stop."

I didn't have much time to answer but within me the song of my soul quietly reverberated,

I have decided to follow Jesus,
Though none go with me,
Still I will follow,
No turning back, No turning back.

From deep in my heart I responded, "I know I have a job to do but I think it is more than just keeping the halls empty between classes and making sure that no fights erupt. I talk to these kids, some smoking marijuana on the way to school or on drugs during school. Some of them are crushed from parents who would be glad to get rid of them. They talk to me as someone who will listen. I know you might prefer that they all come in and talk to you and I am sure some do. But, I am in the halls everyday of every week and they talk to me. I can't get them in trouble. I won't talk to their parents. I just listen and then if they will listen, I tell them something happened to me that I simply cannot deny. Jesus came into my life, a young boy from a broken home doing things that I am too ashamed to admit in this office. Yes, I have a deep hope within me that people's lives can change, kids on drugs, kids in broken homes. I can't commit to you that I will stop sharing. But, I will keep in mind what you have said."

The counselor said nothing and I walked out. He never approached me again. Not all the kids were excited to see me each day as I walked those halls of East Aurora High School but they were all special to me.

CHAPTER 30

The Wedding

After we had received everyone's blessing, we began to plan our wedding. Guys don't have much sense about this kind of stuff but I have been told that women often imagine the day of their wedding. They think about the flowers, the attendants, the wedding dress, all these things. I didn't even have an engagement ring for Judy.

Judy began to look for a church. We wanted to get married before Christmas so we could use the holidays for our honeymoon. Nothing was available. Incredibly, one of the secretaries at Judy's school mentioned that her niece cancelled her wedding on December 18 at St. Theresa Catholic Church. Immediately we called Father Jack who was not aware of the change. He called us back and said we could have the day if we wanted it. That was less than two months away. Judy and I both said yes!

This was not an era of instant everything. With so little time, we had to craft our own invitations and accept offers from friends to help with the preparations. Bev Miller made a lovely wedding dress, Ray took pictures, and her students with disabilities helped with the beverages and seating. Judy's Aunt Marie made the beautiful flower arrangements. Not to mention, Judy looked like a storybook princess. My sister Lucy had curled her hair and the waves beneath her veil flowed like the ocean. Our wedding was mid-afternoon with Will Ogden and Father Jack officiating at St. Theresa Catholic Church on Farnsworth Avenue. We had known each other just two months and we were now being presented to the whole church as Mr. and Mrs. David Valdez. Just as the December snow held on to the tree branches and blades of grass, my bride glistened in the sunlight of a cold winter day. You may now kiss the bride.

Finding a reception hall at such short notice had almost been impossible so we had our reception at Simmons Junior High School cafeteria. Afterward my mom held a mini-reception at her house and then we were off to Judy's parent's house in Bensenville for our third reception. We finally got home to our new apartment about 12 midnight. We inserted the key, quietly turned the lock, but we couldn't get in. Mrs. Putt, our elderly landlady, had pulled the manual deadbolt lock across the door and we were locked out on our wedding night! She didn't remember that we were coming to our new home this night. At 89 years old she probably forgot that this would be our first day in our new apartment. We tried knocking as hard as we could but she was hard of hearing and we were stranded. Panic was beginning to set in.

So there we were well past midnight, Judy in her wedding dress and me in my tuxedo with no place to go. We began to drive around the neighborhood to see if anyone was awake. We could try to call Mrs. Putt on the phone if we could find a place from which to call her. (As of yet cell phones were not invented.) We saw a light on in a house about a few blocks away and so there we were, walking up the sidewalk of some complete strangers in the middle of the night. Now when the people saw that Judy had a wedding dress on and I had a tuxedo, they were not alarmed. They laughed with us when we told them our dilemma, but only after the commiserating, 'Poor Things'. So we called Mrs. Putt who, thank the Lord with angels singing, answered the phone. We went back to our apartment and she opened the door. Mrs. Putt laughed with us and so we began our marriage that day.

CHAPTER 31

Go and Sin No More

We had been married for several months and were living at 423 West Park Avenue. We were deeply in love and things seemed to be perfect. But as I looked around our apartment I was bothered by some items that were in my possession. There were books that were "temporarily on loan" from the University of Illinois. I didn't really borrow them, I took them. I was just stupid and I took them. I have no excuse for myself. I packaged the books up and sent them back. Then, I had a lamp. When I needed a lamp and couldn't afford to buy one, I went into one of the residence halls in the middle of the day, unplugged it and walked out the door. It was that simple. But the Lord was working in my life to make things right. I packed the table lamp and sent it back, too. Judy began to wonder who she married.

"Is there anything else?" Judy said.

I cringed. I knew I had been forgiven. But there were things that I hadn't told her, things for which I had to make restitution. I had been a Christian for barely a year and somehow I was seriously stumbling for words to say.

"Yes, one more thing. When I was 17, one of my close buddies told me that we could break into his friend's house and take some beer out of the refrigerator. No one would be home and his friend would leave a window unlocked which we could climb through. He wanted us to break into his home. I didn't know why. Maybe he was the rebellious type. Well, we not only took the beer but we took some coins."

"Then what happened?" Judy said with the incredulous look that made me want to crawl under the rock that I came from and never come out.

"Somehow the police learned that I was involved. I was asked to come in for questioning and I got arrested and booked."

"You got arrested. And you never told me!" I could tell that Judy was hurt and confused.

"I didn't think about it."

"You didn't think about it!" The quiver in Judy's voice showed the betrayal she felt.

"They let me go and expunged the arrest because they couldn't prove anything. But now I feel I have to confess."

"What are you going to do Dave? What is going to happen to us?"

"I don't know."

Several days later, I went to the police station. I looked at the officer at the front desk and I said, "I need to speak to a detective about a crime I committed several years ago."

I was directed to an office on the second floor of the police station. Each step on those stairs showered pain into my soul as I approached my destination. I whispered to myself,

I have decided to follow Jesus, no turning back, no turning back.

I knocked to get the attention of two detectives who seemed quite busy. They looked up at me, I took a deep breath and I said,

"About 6-7 years ago, when I was in high school I broke into a home and I want to confess to that crime."

"Have you done anything else since?"

"No sir."

One of the police officers turned around, looked straight at me and said,

"Then just go home and forget about it."

Stunned, I walked down those stairs, past the attending officer, and exited the police station. I got in my car and drove home to an anxious wife who was ready to bail me out of jail.

"Tell me what happened. I have to know!"

"You are not going to believe this. God had his hand on me and when I told the two detectives I broke into a house, they just said, forget about it."

"They just said forget about it?" Judy said.

"Yeah, that's it. It was like that story in the Bible where the angel opens the doors of the jail. I just walked out. They didn't even question where it happened or when it happened. Just go home and forget about it. That's all they said."

I recounted the whole story over again from beginning to end. Judy hugged me as we sat on the couch both emotionally drained from the day.

But it wasn't completely over because I had to return those coins to their rightful owner. I couldn't remember the house so I went to the library to look through microfiche of Aurora Beacon News articles in that time period. After looking through about 2 weeks of news clippings I found the address. I asked Judy to go with me to the home. I held her hand as we walked up the driveway. With a box of coins in one hand and my Bible in the other, I knocked on the door and this man answered.

"Sir, I was wondering if I could speak with you just for a moment."

"I don't want to talk with you." He said in an unwieldy tone.

"Sir, please, let me explain. This directly involves you and something I did ..."

"Stay away from me and leave!" He slammed the door in my face. Judy and I looked at each other and walked away.

"Dave, what are you going to do now?" Judy asked.

"I am going to write this man a long letter on how a young man made some stupid mistakes in his life. I am going to tell him how Jesus came into his life and with the letter will be the coins that I had stolen."

"Ok, honey, let's go home," Judy said.

"I could have been in prison but for the grace of God," I said.

"I know," she said in a whispered tone.

We embraced and cried a lot that night. Somehow, we both understood how misdirected young people can make stupid mistakes and pay dearly. No doubt, there were many people out there that had arrest records and convictions for doing less than I had done. So I knew, but for the Grace of God, there I go.

> *At dawn He appeared again in the temple courts, where all the people gathered around Him, and He sat down to teach them. The teachers of the law and the Pharisees brought in a woman caught in adultery. They made her stand before the group and said to Jesus, "Teacher, this woman was caught in the act of adultery. In the Law Moses commanded us to stone such women. Now what do you say?" They were using this question as trap in order to have a basis for accusing Him. But Jesus bent down and started to write on the ground with His finger. When they kept on questioning Him, he straightened up and said to them, "If any one of you is without sin, let him be the first to throw a stone at her." Again he stooped down and wrote on the ground. At this, those who heard began to go away one at a time, the older ones first, until only Jesus was left, with the woman still standing there. Jesus straightened up and asked her, "Woman where are they? Has no one condemned you? "No one, Sir," she said. "Then neither do I condemn you," Jesus declared, "Go, and sin no more." John 8:2-11 NIV*

CHAPTER 32

The Mustard Seed Jesus House

My job at East Aurora Schools was over and the summer of 1972 had begun. Jerry Harvey had received inquiries about a Jesus People tent revival group that wanted to come to Aurora. Christ is the Answer ministries with Bill Lowery were coming to Aurora and we helped them get a city permit to stage the tent in Phillips Park. Hundreds of Jesus People mostly 18-25 year olds came into Aurora and they shared the Gospel at shopping centers, downtown Aurora and wherever they could find an audience. And every night Bill Lowery preached from the Big Top. When groups of young adults went to Northgate Shopping Center to pass out materials, the police started arresting these kids for trespassing. Judy and I went to the shopping center in support but we were not stopped by the police. We learned that the police had arrested so many, they could barely contain them in the city jail. Without bail, they remained incarcerated for the night.

The next day, all those arrested were to appear in court. As Judy and I arrived in support; the courtroom, the hallways, and the entire police station were filled with people singing Amazing Grace. They let everyone go and we rejoiced in the goodness of our Lord. It was at this same time that Jared Worby, the young man I saw at Kresges, joined the tent ministry. He told me how much an impact my testimony had on him. Jared would later start his own tent ministry and travel extensively throughout Eastern Europe especially the areas of Bosnia and Sarajevo.

The Jesus People would be packing their tent soon for their

next destination. Judy and I began to pray whether we should join them. I talked to Will Ogden and he told me that Judy and I were needed in Aurora. I felt this was confirmation for us to stay, but I knew that there was still something more we should be doing in Aurora.

Jerry Harvey and I began to look for a house, not any house, but a huge house that a lot of people could occupy. Jerry and I had seen over and over again young adults coming to know Jesus but quickly falling away. They needed a place where they could get out of their environment and concentrate on following God's plan for their lives.

Jerry found a home at 18 South Root Street, only a few blocks from downtown Aurora. It had a huge living room, dining room, kitchen and porch on the first floor. It had two family units on the second floor and 4 bedrooms on the third floor. We could convert the basement into about 4 bedrooms. Jerry and I talked on how we would buy this gigantic home. Jerry would sell his home and take any equity he had, and Judy and I would take our savings that we had put aside to buy a home. Will Ogden cosigned for the home as they would not sell it to Jerry as he was full time in the ministry and I had insufficient work history. So in 1973 we purchased this gigantic home where single women would live on the third floor and single men in the basement. Jerry and his family, and Judy and I, would live on the two family units on the second floor. We named the house the Mustard Seed Jesus House.

There we began an exhaustive ministry of bringing in young adults. The most we had living there was about 12-14 young adults. After living there for a year Peggy, Jim and Art Silva, my cousins, wanted to come live with us. My Aunt Mary had passed away about two years earlier and they wanted a new home with Judy and I. Peggy, Jim, and Art were 17, 10, and 7. Judy and I weren't yet 25 years old. This was a very hard decision as Judy and I had not yet been married two years. We were fully entrenched in the Mustard Seed Jesus House and we didn't know how to raise a family. We said yes but knew that some big changes had to occur. After being at the Jesus House for less than two years, we bought a house on the West Side of Aurora on Pennsylvania Avenue. There we would raise Peggy, Jim, and Art, and then begin to start our own family.

CHAPTER 33

Fast Forward

The interim between 25 and 65 years of age seemed to pass so quickly. After 7 years of working at Northwestern Chemical, I went to work for a Christian friend named Bob Mack. He owned a small chemical company, S.H. Mack and Company. We made drilling and grinding fluids and lubricants for aluminum can manufacturers. After about 2 years working with him I discussed going back to school part time to get an advanced degree. He was so excited about it that he paid my tuition, my books, and my travel back and forth to school. I worked full time, went to school full time and managed a family with the perseverance of a special wife. I received my Ph.D. in Analytical Chemistry in 1985 at Northern Illinois University specializing in Nuclear Magnetic Resonance Spectroscopy. In God's timing I realized my dreams. In all of that we helped raise Peggy, Jim, and Art, and then our 4 children; Hannah, Thomas, Kristin, and Scott.

After taking at job at Georgia-Pacific as research manager of the analytical chemistry lab, we moved to Georgia in 1989 and attended Grace Fellowship Church in Snellville. I travelled on 5 mission trips, several with my wife and one with my son, Tom, to South America. We did medical missions in Peru and 'Christmas in the Dump' in Ecuador. My good friend, David Williams, was the lead on these trips and without his encouragement I don't know if I would have gone.

As I pondered retirement, I knew that the last mile had to be deeper and that I had to put forth a greater effort to make it real. Judy retired from Gwinnett County Schools and I from Georgia-Pacific. We moved to Ellijay, Georgia about 60 miles north of Atlanta. I wondered how much I would struggle not having the structure of a full time job that consumed my entire day. I know I needed much more than a Sunday Service and a Wednesday Bible study. It seems strange to say that this was exactly how I felt after I turned my heart towards God in 1971.

We were attending Orchard Church when Pastor Steve Dusek said, "We are going to need volunteers all summer for Seamless Summer." What's that, I thought? Pastor Steve continued, "One of the main projects is to provide lunch to underprivileged children in a government funded program at Tower Road. If you are interested see Glenda Murphy."

Our church was spearheading a lunch and activity program for primarily Guatemalan children in our community. I was interested in finding out more so I told my wife that we should go to Tower Road.

The first day we were amazed that there was this type of poverty in Ellijay. Many of the families lived in dilapidated trailers and sometimes multiple families would be in a single trailer. The trailers were repaired with cardboard, plywood and particleboard. I thought back to my own experiences on River Street where I was convinced that I lived in the worst home in all of Aurora, Illinois. But, they had even less than I as a young boy.

After we packed the food in bags and distributed the lunches, I played games with the children; volleyball, jump rope, hopscotch, and bubbles. Most importantly I would talk to the kids and they would tell me about their families. I would talk to them in Spanish when necessary even though my skills weren't that great. Three hours later, I stood there exhausted.

"Mr. Dave, are you coming back tomorrow?" One of the boys asked earnestly.

"I don't know. I will think about it." I hadn't made a commitment other than coming this first day.

"Mr. Dave, aren't you going to come back to see us tomorrow?" came another voice.

"I don't know for sure, but probably," I said in a sincere voice.

"You won't come back, I know you won't." And when I heard this my heart was breaking. I could only think of the many people who had helped me and now I had a chance to help end this cycle here at Tower Road.

"OK, OK, I will be here tomorrow." And I was there the next day, and the day after that, and it stretched out all summer. As Ms. Glenda told me later, she looked in my eyes and knew I was hooked. I developed great relationships not only with the kids but all of my co-workers from our church, Earl and Maria, Janice and Marc, Rod, Cindy, Meg and of course my hero, Glenda Murphy. (And so many more that I have not mentioned.)

One hot summer Georgia day in the high 90s, we had cold watermelon to serve after the lunches. We had served the kids in the outdoor sun until we got some canopy tents. But even under the canopy tents, the heat could be truly devastating. I watched carefully that all the kids had refreshed themselves with ice cold watermelon. We then stopped playing volleyball and I said out loud,

"I sure would like a piece of watermelon!"

I approached the table where Miss Maria was slicing the melons, and unexpectedly one of the kids shouted out as loud as he could,

"Mr. Dave, you don't deserve watermelon."

As he jokingly repeated that louder and louder, I gathered several of the boys around me. I put my arms around them and said,

"You are right, I don't deserve watermelon. I don't deserve the good gifts that I have received in my life. And though I was a sinner deserving only punishment, God came into my life, forgave me and changed me into someone new." And it reminded me of the old Gaither song that when I had nothing to offer, he made something beautiful of my life.

A few days later, we were having watermelon again. One of the small girls came up to me with a piece of watermelon. I looked into her deep brown eyes and said,

"Why did you bring me a piece of watermelon?"

And she said to me, "You looked hot and tired, and you deserved a piece of watermelon."

I didn't know if she had heard me speak to the boys. It didn't matter, my heart melted not from the heat of the day but the warmth of her heart. So my entire summer passed by feeding the kids and sharing the love of Christ when possible. We are now in our second season of Seamless Summer. There are now many new children whom I have come to care for deeply. And I say to them all throughout the summer,

> *Know and love the Lord.*
> *Respect your parents and adults.*
> *Get a good education, study hard.*
> *Be all that you can because you can be leaders.*

And so I have come full circle. I am coming back to the child that I was. I am embracing the love that was given to me so that I might be a vessel of the God that has given all to me. Lord, let me not look with my eyes but let me see love with your eyes. Let me understand how you love. So I have learned …

> *If I speak in the tongues of men and of angels, but have not love, I am only a resounding gong, or a clanging cymbal. If I have the gift of prophecy and can fathom all mysteries and all knowledge, and if I have faith that can move mountains, but have not love, I am nothing. If I give all I posses to the poor and surrender my body to the flames, but have not love, I gain nothing. 1Corinthians 13:1-3 NIV*

CHAPTER 34

The Letters

And now I leave with you one final letter. Not the special letter I received as a second grader from Amy, nor the note from Kathy. I cannot even leave with you the note that Judy wrote to me. These are mine. I hold on to them in my heart as to what is good in this world. They are my anchors to the Lord. They are my history.

It is a letter that maybe you will cherish, maybe one that you will put it your guitar case or in your wallet. Forever, it is yours.

The Love Letter

God knows your heart. He loves you! He knows all your hurts and doubts. He knows your mountains and valleys. Open up the doors of your heart to Him.

He says, "Come."

Your loving friend,

Hallelujah Dave

EPILOGUE

As I wrote this book, I began to call old friends and ask them of some of their recollections. My memories were mostly correct but it was fun to see how at times it differed and I would have to make corrections to the text. It was of great satisfaction to talk to my family and chat about the cities where we lived and the experiences we shared. The laughter and tears were both refreshing and healing.

Most of all, the knowledge that both my Dad and Mom had a relationship with God before they passed on was celebratory to me. My sisters and my brother have a growing relationship with God and I had the amazing privilege of baptizing my brother.

To all my friends from school, the Jesus House years, and my friends from Snellville and Ellijay, Thank You. To my readers, I hope you have enjoyed my story.

To my immediate family and extended family, I hope this book is meaningful and is a blessing for years to come.

Feel free to write me at dave@hallelujahdave.com or see me at www.hallelujahdave.com

Printed in the United States
By Bookmasters